JAIL DIARY

AND OTHER WRITINGS

BESTSELLING NON-FICTION

- Gravity by George Gamow
  Sciences/Physics, ISBN: 9789388118705
- How to Develop Self-Confi. and Pub. Speaking by Dale Carnegie
  Mind, Body & Spirit, ISBN: 9789388118286
- How to Stop Worrying and Start Living by Dale Carnegie
  Mind, Body & Spirit, ISBN: 9789387669161
- How to Win Friends and Influence People by Dale Carnegie
  Self Help/General, ISBN: 9789387669178
- Mein Kampf by Adolf Hitler
  Autobiographies/Leaders, ISBN: 9789387669260
- My Experiments with Truth by Mahatma Gandhi
  Autobiographies/Leaders, ISBN: 9789387669277
- Relativity by Albert Einstein
  Sciences/Physics, ISBN: 9789387669185
- The Art of War by Sun Tzu
  Self Help/Success, ISBN: 9789387669321
- The Diary of a Young Girl by Anne Frank
  Autobiographies/Memoirs, ISBN: 9789387669208
- The Magic of Believing by Claudie Bristol
  Religion/Christianity, ISBN: 9789388118217
- The Miracles of Your Mind by Joseph Murphy
  Mind, Body & Spirit, ISBN: 9789387669215
- The Power of Your Subconscious Mind by Joseph Murphy
  Mind, Body & Spirit, ISBN: 9789387669222
- The Richest Man in Babylon by George S. Clason
  Business & Economics, ISBN: 9789388118354
- Think and Grow Rich by Napoleon Hill
  Self Help/Success, ISBN: 9789387669352

Search the book by its ISBN

JAIL DIARY

And Other Writings

Bhagat Singh

GENERAL PRESS

Published by

GENERAL PRESS

4805/24, Fourth Floor, Krishna House
Ansari Road, Daryaganj, New Delhi - 110002
Ph : 011-23282971, 45795759
E-mail : generalpressindia@gmail.com

www.generalpress.in

First Edition : 2021

ISBN : 9789390492084

Published by Azeem Ahmad Khan for General Press

Contents

The Problem of Punjab's Language and Script[1]

February 28, 1933

"An acquaintance of the literature of a society or a country is of prime importance for the understanding of that society or country, because the consciousness of the soul of a society or country, because the consciousness of the soul of a society gets reflected in its literature also." History is witness to the authenticity of the above statement. Countries have followed the direction determined by the flow of their literature. Every nation needs literature of high quality for its own uplift. As literature of a country attains new heights, the country also develops. Patriots – be they merely social reformers or political leaders – pay highest attention to the literature of their country. If they do not create new literature to meet

1. The Punjab Hindi Sahitya Sammelan had organised an essay competition on the above subject in 1923. It was for that competition that Bhagat Singh wrote this article. The General Secretary of Sahitya Sammelan, Shri Bhim Sen Vidyalankar (now expired) liked the article much and preserved it. Bhagat Singh got a prize of Rs. 50 for this article. Subsequently, it was published in *Hindi Sandesh* on February 28, 1933.

the requirements of the contemporary issues and situations, all of their efforts will fail and their work will prove unstable.

Perhaps Garibaldi could not have succeeded in mobilising the army with such ease if Mazzini had not invested his thirty years in his mission of cultural and literary renaissance. The revival of Irish language was attempted with the same enthusiasm along with the renaissance in Ireland. The rulers so much wanted to suppress their language for the ultimate suppression of the Irish people that even kids were punished for the crime of keeping a few verses in Gaelic. The French revolution would have been impossible without the literature of Rousseau and Voltaire. Had Tolstoy, Karl Marx and Maxim Gorky not invested years of their lives in the creation of a new literature, the Russian Revolution would not have taken place, leave alone the propagation and practice of communism.

The same applies to the social and religious reformers. Kabir's ideas have a stable impact because of his literature. Till date, the sweetness and sensitivity of his poems prove captivating to the people.

Exactly the same can be said about Guru Nanak Devji, When the Sikh Gurus started establishing their new order along with the preaching of their beliefs, they felt the need of a new literature and this inspired Guru Angad Devji to evolve the Gurumukhi script. Centuries of continuous warfare and Muslim invasions had dried up the literature of Punjab. The Hindi language was at the verge of extinction. He adopted the Kashmiri script in his search for an Indian language. Later the Adi Granth was compiled by Guru Arjun Devji and Bhai Gurudasji. They took a far-reaching and useful step in this act of creating their own script and literature to perpetuate their beliefs.

Afterwards, as situations changed, the flow of literature also changed. The ceaseless sacrifices and sufferings of the Gurus changed the situation. Whereas we find devotion and self-oblivion in the preaching of the first Guru, and experience a sense of self-effacement in the following couplet:

Nanak nanhe ho rahe, jaisi nanhi doob.
Aur ghas jari jaat hai, doob khoob ki khoob

(Nanak asks all to be as humble and insignificant as the doob grass. While all other grasses are burnt down, doob continues to flourish.)

We find a sense of fellow-feeling and helpfulness for the oppressed in the preaching of Guru Shri Teg Bahadurji:

Baanhi jinhan di pakadiye, sir dijiye baanhi na chhodye,
Guru Teg Bahadur bolya, dharati pai dharam na chodye.

(Whomsoever you provide protection, you should be prepared to sacrifice yourself but not that protection. Guru Teg Bahadur asks you not to forsake your religion on this earth.)

After his sacrifice, suddenly, we sense a warrior spirit in the preaching of Guru Gobind Singhji. When he realised that a mere spiritual devotion could not do anything, he started Chandi worship and turned Sikh community into a community of worshippers and warriors by synthesising spiritualism and fighting. We find in his poems (literature) a new spirit. He writes:

Je tohi prem khelan da chav, sir dhar tali gali mori aav,
Je it maarag pair dharijai, sir dijai kaan no dijai.

(If you are interested in playing the game of love, put your head on your palm and then only enter my lane. In case you put your feet on this path don't fall back, even if you have to lose your life.) And then:

Soora so pahchaniye, je lade deen ke het,
Purja-purja kat mare, kabhu na chhade khet.

(Only he is brave who fights for the cause of the poor. He may be cut into pieces and may be killed, but he should not leave the field.)

And then suddenly, the sword-worship starts.

Carrying the same spirit Baba Banda and others fought Muslim ruler ceaselessly. We find later that when Sikhs are reduced to mere groups of anarchists, declared outlaws, and were continuously compelled to be confined to the forests, no new literature could be created. They had a warrior spirit, a sense of courage and sacrifice and a spirit to continue their war against Muslim rulers, but they could not chalk out their future beyond this. This explains why these warrior groups fought among themselves. It is here that their lack of contemporary spirit worries us. If a warrior and shrewd ruler like Ranjit Singh had not emerged afterwards, Sikhs would have gone down bereft of any high ideal or spirit to have mobilised them.

Along with all this, one more point deserves attention. All the Sanskrit literature, put together, failed to revive the Hindu society; new literature had to be written in a contemporary modern language. Till date, we feel only the effect which was created by that literature of contemporary spirit. Even for a person of proper education and comprehension, the hymns of unintelligible

Sanskrit and ayat (verses) of classical Arabic cannot be as enthusing as is possible by the simple statements in a simple language.

A short history of Punjabi language and literature is sketched out above. Now we turn to our times. Swami Vivekananda in Bengal and Swami Ramtirtha in Punjab were born approximately at the same time. Both were 'great' in the same sense. Both got fame for establishing Indian metaphysics abroad. Swami Vivekanand's mission became a permanent institution in Bengal while Punjab misses a memorial to Swami Ramtirtha. In spite of having significant differences in their thinking, we find strong similarities at the roots. Whereas Swami Vivekananda was preaching Karma Yoga, Swami Ramtirtha was singing in blissfulness:

Ham rukhe tukade khayenge,
Bharat par ware jayenge,
Hum sukhe chane chabayenge,
Bharat ki baat banyenge,
Ham nange umar bitayenge,
Bharat par jaan mitayenge.

(We shall subsist on crumbs but sacrifice ourselves for Bharat. We shall eat the most ordinary food, but work for our country. We shall go naked the whole life, but offer our lives for Bharat.)

Several times, he wept while seeing the setting sun in America, and said:" Now you are rising in my beloved country. Drop my tears like dew-drops over beautiful water-fed fields of India." Such a great devotee of the country and God was born in our province and, if we do not have even a single memorial to him, what else could explain that, except our literary backwardness?

This we feel at every step. Many great men born in Punjab, who are comparable to Shri Devendra Thakur and Keshav Chandra Sen of Bengal, but we did not respect them and easily forgot them after their deaths – for example, guru Gyan Singhji, etc. We find only one reason on bottom, and that is the total lack of literacy interest and awakening, The truth is that no country or community can progress without its literature. But language is the primary need of literature and this is absent in Punjab. In spite of releasing this handicap for long, the question of language has still remained unresolved. The main reason behind this is the unfortunate communalisation of language in our province, in other provinces, we find that Muslims have fully adopted their provincial languages. In the literary world of Bengal. Poet Nazrul-Islam is a shining star. Latif Hussain 'Natwar' is prominent among the Hindi poets. The same is true of Gujrat also. But Punjab is unfortunate. Here, even Hindus and Sikhs are not united, leave the Muslims alone.

Punjab should have been the language of Punjab, like other provinces, but since this has not happened, as this question is a spontaneous question, Muslims have adopted Urdu. Muslims totally lack Indianness, therefore they want to propagate Arabic script and Persian language. While failing to understand the importance of Indianness in the whole of India, they fail to understand the importance of one language, which could only be Hindi. That is why they keep repeating the demand for Urdu like a parrot and take an isolated position.

Then comes the turn of the Sikhs. Their whole literature is in the Gurumukhi script. Hindi is very much there as a component, but Punjabi constitutes the main component. Therefore, the Sikhs adopted Punjabi written in Gurmukhi as their language.

They could not leave that at any cost. They embraced that by making it a communal language.

The Arya Samaj emerged on the other side. Swami Dayanand propagated the feeling for the spread of Hindi throughout Bharatvarsha. Hindi became a religious component of the Arya Samaj movement. These religious attachments benefited the language in one way. That is, while Sikh staunchness secured Punjabi, the insistence of Arya Samajists helped Hindi secure a place of its own.

In the early days of Arya Samaj movement, the Sikhs and Arya Samajists used to have religious gathering at the same place. At that time they had no feelings of being different, but afterwards, a few sentences of Satyartha Prakash caused malice and mutual hatred. The Sikhs, swept in the same stream, started hating even Hindi as well. Other did not take even notice of it.

Afterwards, it is said, a Samaji leader, Mahatma Hansraj Ji held consultations with many leaders and proposed that if they accept the Hindi script, he would get the Punjabi language in Hindi script, and he would get the Punjabi language in Hindi script recognised in the University. But they could not understand the importance of this proposal because of their narrow-mindedness and absence of literary awareness. At this moment, three views prevail in Punjab. Firstly, there is strong attachment for urdu among the Muslims; secondly, for Hindi among Arya Samajis and certain other Hindus; and thirdly, for Punjabi.

It will not be important here to deal with all the languages one by one. First of all, we shall consider the Muslims view. They are staunch supporters of Urdu. At the present time, this language is dominant in Punjab. This is also the language of the court. Then some Muslims say that Urdu scripts saves space. This may be quite right, but the most important question before us at this juncture is to make India a unified nation, but this cannot be done all at once.

For this we have to move step by step. If we cannot adopt one language for the whole of India at the moment, we should at least adopt one script. The urdu script cannot be called a perfect one and the most important point is that it is based on the Persian language. The flights of imagination of urdu poets – even if they are Hindi (Indian) – reach the saaqis (bar-maids) of Persia and date palms of the Arbs countries. Kazi Nazrul-Islam's poems refer to Dhurjate, Vishwamitra and Durvasa quite frequently, but our Punjabi Hindi-Urdu poets could not even think of them. Is it not a matter which makes one sad? Their ignorance of Indianness and Indian literature is the main reason of this. When they cannot imbibe Indianness, how can their literature make us Indian? Students confined to the study of urdu cannot attain the knowledge of the classical literature of India. It is not that these texts cannot be translated into a literary language like urdu, but it will be useful only to a Persian in his pursuit concerning Indian literature.

It will Suffice to say in support of the above statement that when simple words like Arya and Swarajya are written as 'Ariya' and 'Swarajia', what will happen to the deep metaphysical topics? Only a few days back, a government translator, using the urdu script, mistook sage Nachiketa as 'Neechi Kutia' which can be translated as a 'bitch of low origin', while translating an Urdu book Qaumen kis Tarah Zinda Rah Sakti Hain (How nationalities can survive) by Lala Hardayalji, M.A. It was neither Lalaji's fault nor the translator. It was only a shortcoming of the Urdu script and the dissimilarity between Urdu and Hindi languages and literature.

Indian languages and script prevail in the rest of India. In such a situation, should we get absolutely isolated from India point is that, among Muslim writers, the staunch supporters of Urdu write highly Persianised Urdu. The Muslim newspapers like Zamindar and Siyasat have strong Arabic influence which is quite incomprehensible to common people. How can this be propagated in such a situation? We wish our Muslim brothers, while sticking to their religion, think of Indianising themselves like Kamal the Turk. India's salvation is possible only that way. Instead of making language a communal question, we should adopt a wide perspective.

We will now return to the problem of Hindi and Punjabi. Many idealists entertain a vision of the world turned into one single nation, one global nation. This ideal is beautiful and one should keep it before oneself. But this cannot be achieved today; all of our steps, all of our efforts should be directed towards enhancement of happiness by uniting all nationalities, countries and nations into one strong bond. Before that, we have to realise that ideal in our own country. We have to adopt one language, one script, one literature, one ideal and one nation, but the adoption of a single language precedes all the other unities, so they we can communicate with and comprehend each other. A Punjabi and a Madrasi must not sit together mute at a gathering, but try to communicate their ideas and emotions, and this should be done in our own language, Hindi, rather than in an alien language like English. Even this ideal will take years to be realised. First of all, we should create literary awareness in this endeavor, not among a few but in the masses. The people's own language is essential for creating literary awareness among the people. On the basis of this logic, we say that you can succeed in Punjab only in Punjabi language.

Till now, Punjabi has not been able to become a literary language of the central Punjab. It is written in the Gurmukhi script and is now Known as Punjabi. It is neither widely prevalent nor has any literature or scientific significance. It was left unattended earlier, but even now the deficiency of its script disturbs those who are now attending to it. All the words, cannot end without the sound 'a' and its inability to write compound letter; even the word 'Poorna' (complete) cannot be written. This script is thus even more incomplete than Urdu, but when we already have a scientific and perfect Hindi script, what is there to feel hesitant about adopting it? The Gurmukhi script is only distorted form of the Hindi script. Right from the start all the rules are same, then, how much will we be benefited by our immediate switch over to this. The Punjabi language will start developing immediately by adopting this perfect script. And there is no problem in the propagation of it. Hindu women of Punjab already know this script. The DAV school and Sanatan Dharma schools teach only in Hindi, what could be the problem in such a situation? We shall plead with the supporters of Hindi that, ultimately and certainly, only Hindi will be the language of the whole Bharat, but it will be more convenient to propagate it from now on. Punjabi will become like Hindi by adopting the script and then all the differences will disappear; and it is desirable, too that common people could be educated which is possible only through our own language in our own script. See this Punjabi poem:

O rahiya rahe jandya, sun ja gall meri
Sir to pag tere balait di, ihnun fuk muatara la.

(O passerby, listen to me. Burn that foreign turban which thou art wearing on thy head, And take to 'Muatara'.)

Even beautiful Hindi poems cannot cast an impression comparable to this, as they have not yet made a place right in the hearts of the people. They still seem somewhat alien. It is so because Hindi is based on Sanskrit. And the Punjab has gone farther away from that. Persian has maintained its dominance in Punjab to a large extent. For example, a collection of things become 'cheezan' here instead of 'cheezain'. This principle prevails throughout. What is being emphasised here is that Hindi is still far from Punjabi heart in spite of being close to Punjabi; of course, Punjabi will come closer to Hindi when it will adopt the Hindi script attempt creating its literature.

By now almost every major issue has been discussed here. Only one thing now remains to be said. Many people argue that the Punjabi language lacks sweetness, beauty and emotions. This is absolutely baseless. Only recently the sweetness, beauty and emotions. This is absolutely baseless. Only recently the sweetness, beauty and emotions of this song hypnotised Kavindra Ravindra:

Lachhiye, jitthe tu pani doliya,
Utthe ug paye sandal de boote.

(O Lachhi, where you split water at that place sandlewood trees have sprouted.)

Many more examples could be cited. Is the following couplet even the least inferior to the poems of any other language?

Pipal de pattya ve kehi khadkhad layee ae,
Patte jhade purane hun rut navayan di aayee ae.

(Pipal leaves, why are you making noise? The old leaves have fallen and the season for new leaves has come.)

And when Punjab is sitting alone or in the group, will any other language move them to the extent these lines of Gauhar can:

Lam lakkhan to karoran de shah vekhe
Na musafiran koi udhar dende,
Dine raatin de kuch dere,
Na unhan gulan di vasana te
Bhauren bahande gulan di vasana te
Na sappan de muhan te koi pyar denda,
Gauhar same salook han jyuadya de
Moyan giyan un tar koi visar denda.

(I have seen armies of lakhs of millionaires. No one gives loan to the passers-by who never stay, never reside at one place. No one trusts them. Black beetles sit on flowers because of their smell. No one gives love at the hoods of the snakes. O Gauhar, good behavior and welcome is for those who are alive, but everyone says good-bye at the time of death.)

Jeev jyudiyan nu kyon marna ae
Jekar nahintu moyan nn jiaun joga,
Ghar aaye sawali nu kyon ghurna ae
Jekar nahin tu hatthin khair joga;
Mile dilan naun kayaker todna ae
Mile dilan tu bichhadyan nu milaun joga,
Gauhar barhiya rakh band khaane
Jekar nahin tu nekiyan kumaun joga.

(Why kill living beings when you are not able to bring the dead back to life? Why do you stare at the beggar who has come to your door when you are not able to give him something? Why break the union of hearts if you are not able to reunite hearts that are separated? O Gauhar, if you cannot do go to others, then keep your good food and room closed.)

And nowadays brilliant poets like Dard, Mastana, Dewana are enriching the Punjabi's poetry.

It is a pity that such a sweet, such a captivating language has not been adopted even by the Punjabis themselves. They still refuse; and this is the crux of the problem. Everyone backs his arguments on the basis of religious convictions. The only problem concerning the language and script of Punjab is to remove this obstruction, but the hope lies in the increasing literary awareness among the sikhs. Hindu also have it. Why not at all well-meaning people decide by mutual deliberations? This is the only way to arrive at a solution. The question can be attended to by renouncing religious considerations. It should be attempted accordingly and the recognition of Punjabi language of a journal like Prem of Amritsar. This way the problem is resolved. After the elimination of this irritant, Punjab will have such beautiful and 'quality' literature that it will also be counted among the good language of India.

Blood Sprinkled on the Day of Holi Babbar Akalis on the Crucifix

March 15, 1925

[In 1925-26 Bhagat Singh was at Kanpur, working under Ganesh Shankar Vidharthi in the Hindi weekly Partap. While at Kanpur he wrote this article, signing it "Ek Punjabi Yuvak" (a Punjabi youth), about the martyrs of Banbbar Akali movement. It was published in Pratap on March 15, 1926.]

On the day of Holi, February 27, 1926, when we were getting high on our enjoyment, a terrible thing was happening in a corner of this great province. When you will hear it, you will shudder! You will tremble! On that day, six brave Babbar Akalis were hanged in the Lahore Central Jail. Shri kishan Singhji Gadagajja, Shri Santa Singhji, Shri Dilip Sinhghji, Shri Nand Singhji, Shri Karam Singhji and Shri Dharam Singhji, had been showing a great indifference to the trial for the last two years, which speaks of their fond waiting for this day. After months, the judge gave his verdict. Five to be hanged, many for life imprisonment or exile, and sentences of very long imprisonments. The accused heroes thundered. Even the skies echoed with their triumphant slogans. Then an appeal was prefered. Instead of five, now six were sent to the noose. The same day the news came that a mercy petition was sent. The Punjab Secretary declared that the hanging would be put off. We were waiting but, all of a sudden, on the very day of Holi, we saw a small contingent of mourners carrying the dead bodies of the heroes towards the cremation site. Then last rites were completed quietly.

The city was still celebrating. Colour was still being thrown on the passers-by. What a terrible indifference. If they were misguided, if they were frenzied, let them be so. They were fearless patriots, in any case. Whatever they did, they did it for this wretched country. They could not bear injustice. They could not countenance the fallen nation. The oppression on the poor people became insufferable for them. They could not tolerate exploitation of the masses, they challenged and jumped into action. They were full of life. Oh! the terrible toll of their dedicated deeds! You are blessed! After the death, friends and foes are all alike-this is the ideal of men. Even if they might have done something hateful, their lives at the altar of our nation, is something to the opposite side, could highly and uninhibitedly appreciate the courage, patriotism and commitment of the brave revolutionary of Bengal, Jatin Mukherjee, while mourning his death. But we the cowards and human wretches lack the courage of even sighing and putting off our celebrations even for a moment. What a disheartening deed! The poor! they were given the "adequate" punishment even by the standard of the brutal bureaucrats. An act of a terrible tragedy thus ended, but the curtain is not down as yet. The drama will have some more terrible scenes. The story is quite lengthy, we have to turn back a little to know about it.

The Non-Cooperation Movement was at its peak. The Punjab did not lag behind. The Sikhs also rose from their deep slumber and it was quite an awakening. The Akali Movement was started. Sacrifices were made in abundance. Master Mota Singh, ex-teacher of Khalsa Middle School, Mahalpur (district Hoshiarpur), delivered a speech. A warrant was issued against him, but the idea of availing of the hospitality of the crown did not find his favour. He was against offering arrest to fill the jails. His speeches still continued. In Kot-Phatuhi village, a big 'Deevan' was called. Police cordoned the area off from all sides; even then Master Mota Singh delivered his speech. The whole audience stood up and dispersed on the orders of the persident of the meeting. The Master escaped mysteriously. This hide-and-seek continued for long. The government was in a frenzy. At last, a friend turned traitor, and Master Saheb was arrested after a year and a half. This was the first scene of that horrible drama.

The "Guru ka bagh" movement was started. The hired hoodlums were there to attack the unarmed heroes and to beat them half-dead. Could anyone who looked at or listened to this, help being mover? It was a case of arrests and arrests everywhere. A warrant was also issued against Sardar Kishan Singhji Gadagajja, but he also belonged to the same category and did not offer arrest. The police strained all its nerves but he always escaped. He had an organisation of his own. He could not bear the violence against unarmed agitators. He felt the need of using arms along with this peaceful movement.

On the one hand, the dogs, the hunting dogs of the government, were searching for the clues, to get his scent; on the other, it was decided to "reform" the sycophants (Jholi Chukkas). Sardar Kishan Singhji used to say that we must keep ourselves armed for our own security, but we should not take any precipitate action for the time being. The majority was against this. At last, it was decided that three of them should give their names, take all the blame on themselves and start reforming these sycophants. Sardar Karam Singhji, Sardar Dhanna Singhji and Sardar Uday Singhji stepped forward. Just keep aside the question of its propriety for a moment and imagine the scene when they took the oath:

> We will sacrifice our all in the service of the country. We swear to die fighting but not to go to the prison.

What a beautiful, sanctified scene it must have been, when these people who had given up all of their family affections, were taking such an oath! Where is the end of sacrifice? Where is the limit to courage and fearlessness? Where does the extremity of idealism reside?

Near a station on Shyam Churasi-Hoshiarpur railway branch line, a Subedar became the first victim. After that, all these three declared their names. The government tried its best to arrest them, but failed. Sardar Kishan Singh Gadagajja was once almost trapped by the police near Roorki Kalan. A young man who accompanied him, fell down after getting injured, and was captured. But even there, Kishan Singhji escaped with the help of his arms. He met a Sadhu on the way who told him about a herb in his possession which could materialise all his plans and work miracles. Sardarji believed him and visited this Sadhu unarmed. The Sadhu gave him some herbs to prepare and brought the police in the meanwhile. Sardar Saheb was arrested. That Sadhu was an inspector of the CID department. The Babbar Akalis stepped up their activities. Many pro-government men were killed. The doab land lying in between Beas and Sutlej, that is, the districts of Jullundur and Hoshiarpur, had been there on the political map of the country, even before this. The majority of martyrs of 1915 belonged to these districts.

Now again, there was the upheaval. The police department used all its power at its command, which proved quite useless. There is a small river near Jullundur; "Chaunta Sahib" Gurudwara is located there in a village on the banks of the river. There Shri Karam Singhji, Shri Dhanna Singhji, Shri Uday Singhji and Shri Anoop Singhji were sitting with a few others, preparing tea. All of a sudden, Shri Dhanna Singhji said: "Baba Karam Singhji! We should at once leave this place. I sense something very inauspicious happening." The 75-year old Sardar Karam Singh showed total indifference, but Shri Dhanna Singhji left the place, along with his 18-year old follower Dilip Singh. Quite suddenly Baba Karam Singh stared at Anoop Singh and said: "Anoop Singh, you are not a good person", but after this, he himself became unmindful of his own premonition. They were still talking when police made a declaration: Send out the rebels, otherwise the village will be burnt down. But the villagers did not yield.

Seeing all this, they themselves came out. Anoop Singh ran with all the bombs and surrendered. The remaining four people were standing, surrounded from all sides. The British police captain said: "Karam Singh! drop the weapons and you will be pardoned." The hero responded challengingly: "We will die a martyr's death while fighting, as a real revolutionary, for the sake of our motherland, but we shall not surrender our weapons." He inspiringly called his comrades. They also roared like lions. A fight ensued. Bullets flew in all directions. After their ammunition exhausted, these brave people jumped into the river and bravely died after hours of ceaseless fighting.

Sardar Karam Singh was 75 years old. He had been in Canada. His character was pure and behaviour ideal. The government concluded that the Babbar Akalis were finished, but actually they grew in strength. The 18-year old Dilip Singh was a very handsome and strong, well-built, though illiterate, young man. He had joined some dacoit gang. His association with Shri Dhanna Singhji turned him from a dacoit into a real revolutionary. Many notorious dacoits like Banta Singh and Variyam Singh, too, gave up dacoity and joined them.

There were not afraid of death. They were eager to wash their old sins. They were increasing in number day-by-day. One day when Dhanna Singh was sitting in a village named. Mauhana, the police was called. Dhanna Singh was down with drinks and caught without resistance. His revolver was snatched, he was handcuffed and brought out. Twelve policemen and two British officers had surrounded him. Exactly at that moment there was a thunderous noise of explosion. It was the bomb exploded by Dhanna Singhji. He died on the spot along with one British officer and ten policemen. All the rest were badly wounded.

In the same fashion, Banta Singh, Jwala Singh and some others were surrounded in a village named Munder. They all were gathered on the roof of a house. Short were fired, a cross-fire ensued for some time, but then the police sprinkled kerosene oil by a pump and put the house on fire. Banta Singh was killed there, but Variyam Singh escaped even from there.

It will not be improper here to describe a few more similar incidents. Banta Singh was a very courageous man. Once he snatched a horse and a rifle from the guard of the armoury in the Jullundur Cantonment. Those days several police squads were desperately looking for him; one such squad confronted him somewhere in the forest. Sardar Saheb challenged them immediately: "If you have courage, come and confront me." On that side, there were slaves of money; on this side, the willing sacrifice of life. There was no comparison of motives. The police squad beat a retreat.

This was the condition of the special police squads deputed to arrest them. Anyway, arrests had become a routine. Police check-posts were erected in almost every village. Gradually, the Babbar Akalis were weakened. Till now it had seemed as if they were the virtual rulers. Wherever they happened to be visiting, they were warmly hosted, by some with fear and terror. The supporters of the regime were defeatist. They lacked the courage to move out of their residences between the sunset and the sunrise. They were the 'heroes' of the time. They were brave and their worship was believed to be a kind of hero-worship, but gradually they lost their strength. Hundreds among them were imprisoned, and cases were instituted against them.

Variyam Singh was the lone survivor. He was moving towards Layallpur, as the pressure of police had increased in Jullundur and Hoshiarpur. One day he was hopelessly surrounded there, but he came out fighting valiantly. He was very much exhausted. He was alone. It was a strange situation. One day he visited his maternal uncle in the village named Dhesian. Arms were kept outside. After taking his meals, he was moving towards his weaponry when the police arrived. He was surrounded. The British officer caught him from the backside. He wounded him badly with his kripan (sward), and he fell down. All the efforts to handcuff him failed. After two years of suppression, the Akali Jatha came to an end. Then the cases started, one of which has been discussed above. Quite recently too, they had wished to be hanged soon. Their wish has been fulfilled; they are now quiet.

Beware, Ye Bureaucracy

December 18, 1928

[A handwritten leaflet explaining the reasons for Saunders' murder, written on December 18, 1928 on Mozang House den and pasted at several places on the walls of Lahore in the night between the 18th and 19th. A copy in Bhagat Singh's handwriting was produced as an exhibit in the Lahore Conspiracy Case.]

Hindustan Socialist Republican Army Notice

J.P. Sunders is dead; Lala Lajpat Rai is avenged

Really it is horrible to imagine that so lowly and violent hand violent hand of an ordinary Police Official, J.P. Saunders could ever dare to touch in such an insulting way the body of one so old, so revered and so loved by 300 millions of people of Hindustan and thus cause his death. The youth and manhood of India was challenged by blows hurled down on the head of the India's nationhood. And let the world know that India still lives; that the blood of youths has not been totally cooled down and that they can still risk their lives, if the honour of their nation is at stake. And it is proved through this act by those obscure who are ever persecuted, condemned and denounced even by their own people.

Beware, Ye Tyrants; Beware

Do not injure the felling of a downtrodden and oppressed country. Think twice before perpetrating such diabolical deed, And remember that despite 'Arms Act' and strict guards against the smuggling of arms, the revolvers will ever continue to flow in-if no sufficient at present for and armed revolt, then at least sufficient to avenge the national insults. Inspite of all the denunciations and condemnation 0f their own kiths and kins, and ruthless repression and persecution of the alien government, party of young men will ever live to teach a lesson to the haughty rulers. They will be so bold as to cry even amidst the raging storm of opposition and repression, even on the scaffold:

"LONG LIVE THE REVOLUTION"!

Sorry for the death of a man. But in this man has died the representative of an institution which is so cruel, lowly and so base that it must be abolished. In this man has died an agent of the British authority in India – the most tyrannical of Govt. of Govts. In the world.

Sorry for the bloodshed of a human being; but the sacrifice of individuals at the altar of the Revolution that will bring freedom to all and make the exploitation of man by main impossible, is inevitable.

Long Live The Revolution"!

Sd/ - Balraj

Dated

18th December, 1928

Letter to Shaheed Sukhdev[2]

April 5, 1929

Dear Brother,

By the time you receive this letter I will be gone, going to a far off destination. Let me assure that I am prepared for the voyage in spite of all the sweet memory and in spite of all the charms of my life here. Up to this day one thing pinched in my heart and it was this that my brother, my own brother, misunderstood and accused me of a very serious charge – the charge of weakness. Today I am quite satisfied, today more than ever do I feel that was nothing, but a misunderstanding, a wrong calculation. My overfrankness was interpreted as my talkativeness, and my confession as my weakness. And now I feel it was misunderstanding and only is understanding. I am not weak, not weaker than anyone amongst us, brother. With a clear heart I go, will you clear too? It will be very kind of you. But note that you are to take no hasty step,

2. This letter deals with the views of Bhagat Singh on the question of love and sacrifice in the life of a revolutionary. It was written on April 5, 1929 in Sita Ram Bazar House, Delhi. The letter was taken to Lahore by Shri Shiv Verma and handed over to Sukhdev. It was recovered from him at the time of his arrest on April 13 and was produced as one of the exhbits in Lahore Conspiracy Case.

soberly and calmly you are to carry on the work. Don't try to take the chance at the very outset. You have some duty towards the public, and that you can fulfill by continuing this work. As a suggestion I would say that M.R. Shastri appeals to me more than ever. Try to bring him in the arena, provided he himself may be willing, clearly knowing the dark future. Let him mix with men and study their psychology. If he will work in the right spirit, he will be the better judge. Arrange as you may deem fit. Now, brother, let us be happy.

By the way, I am say that I cannot help arguing once again my case in the matter under discussion. Again do I emphasise that I am full of ambition and hope and of full charm of life. But I can renounce all at the time of need, and that is the real sacrifice. These things can never be hinderance in the way of man, provided he be a man. You will have the practical proof in the near future. While discussing anybody's character you asked me one thing, whether love ever proved helpful to any man. Yes, I answer that question today. To Mazzini it was. You must have read that after the utter failure and crushing defeat of his first rising he could not bear the misery and haunting ideas of his dead comrades. He would have gone mad or committed suicide but for one letter of a girl he loved. He would as strong as any one, nay stronger than all. As regards the moral status of love I may say that it in itself is nothing BUT PASSION, not an animal passion but a human one, and very sweet too. Love in itself can never be an animal passion. Love always elevates the character of man. It never lowers him, provided love be love. You can't call these girls – mad people, as we generally see in films – lovers. They always play in the hands of animals passions. The true love cannot be created. It comes of its own accord, nobody can say when. It is but natural. And I may tell you that a young man and a young girl can love each other, and with the aid of their love they can overcome the passions themselves and can maintain their purity. I may clear one thing here; when I said that love has human weakness, I did not say it for an ordinary human being at this stage, where the people generally are. But that is most idealistic stage when man would overcome all these sentiments, the love, the hatred, and so on. When man will take reason as the sole basis of his activity. But at present it is not bad, rather good and useful to man. And moreover while rebuking the love. I rebuked the love of one individual for one, and that too in idealistic stage. And even then, man must have the strongest feelings of love which he may not confine to one individual and may make it universal. Now I think I have cleared my position. One thing I may tell you to mark; we in spite of all radical ideas that we cherish, have not been able to do away with the over idealistic Arya Samajist conception of morality. We may talk glibly about all the radical things that can possible be conceived, but in practical life we begin to tremble at the very outset. This I will request you do away with. And may I, Without fear at all the misapprehension in my mind, request you do kindly lower the standard of your over-idealism a bit, not to be harsh to those who will live behind and will be the victims of a disease as myself? Don't rebuke them and thus add to their woes and miseries. They need your sympathy. May I repeat that you, without bearing any sort of grudge against any particular individual, will sympathise with those who needed the most? But you cannot realise these things unless and until you yourself fall a victim to this. But, why I am writing all this? I wanted to be frank. I have cleared my heart.

Wish you all success and happy life.

Yours, B.S

The Red Pamphlet[3]

April 8, 1929

On the 8th April, 1929, the Viceroy's proclamation, enacting the two Bills, was to be made, despite the fact that the majority of members were opposed to it, and had rather rejected in earlier.

The Hindustan Socialist Republican Army (Notice)

It takes a loud voice to make the deaf hear, with these immortal words uttered on a similar occasion by Valiant, a French anarchist martyr, do we strongly justify this action of ours.

Without repeating the humiliating history of the past ten years of the working of the reforms (Montague-Chelmsford Reforms) and without mentioning the insults hurled at the Indian nation through this House-the so-called Indian Parliament-we want to point out that, while the people expecting some more crumbs of reforms from the Simon Commission, and are ever quarreling

3. This document was primarily written by Bhagat Singh. On April 8, 1929, Bhagat Singh and Batukeshwar Dutt showered copies of the leaflet on the floor of Central Assembly Hall in New Delhi after tossing two bombs into the Assembly Hall corridors.

over the distribution of the expected bones, the Government is thrusting upon us new repressive measures like the Public Safety and the Trade Disputes Bill, while reserving the Press Sedition Bill for the next session. The indiscriminate arrests of labour leaders working in the open field clearly indicate whither the wind blows.

In these extremely provocative circumstances, the Hindustan Socialist Republican Association, in all seriousness, realizing their full responsibility, had decided and ordered its army to do this particular action, so that a stop be put to this humiliating farce and to let the alien bureaucratic exploiters do what they wish, but they must be made to come before the public eve in their naked form.

Let the representatives of the people return to their constituencies and prepare the masses for the coming revolution, and let the Government know that while protesting against the Public Safety and Trade Disputes Bills and the callous murder of Lala Lajpat Rai, on behalf of the helpless Indian masses, we want to emphasize the lesson often repeated by history, that it is easy to kill individuals but you cannot kill the ideas. Great empires crumbled while the ideas survived, Bourbons and Czars fell, while the revolution marched ahead triumphantly.

We are sorry to admit that we who attach so great a sanctity to human life, who dream of a glorious future, when man will be enjoying perfect peace and full liberty, have been forced to shed human blood. But the sacrifice of individuals at the altar of the 'Great Revolution' that will bring freedom to all, rendering the exploitation of man by man impossible, is inevitable.

"Long Live the Revolution."[4]

Signed,
Balraj[5]
Commander-in-Chief

---

4. This phrase (translated from "*Inquilab Zindabad!*") became one of the most enduring slogans of the Indian Independence Movement. Bhagat Singh and Batukeshwar Dutta repeated the slogan at their June 1929 trial on charges related to the bomb-throwing incident.
5. "Balraj" was the pen name for the Commander-in-chief of the Hindustan Socialist Republican Army, Chander Shekhar Azad.

Letter to Superintendent, CID

The letter itself bears no date, but one of the annotations made on it by officials provides a date of 31 May 1929.

The Superintendent (Special Duty)
C.I.D. (Political Branch)
Lahore

Dear Sir,

I will feel much obliged if you will kindly allow me to have an interview with my father, as I have got some very important instructions to give him for my defense counsel in connection with the Delhi case.

I hope you will not disallow it on the grounds that I have already had an interview, because the matter is very urgent.

Hoping to be favoured,

Yours Etc.

Bhagat Singh

Joint Statement

Full Text of Statement of S. Bhagat Singh and B.K. Dutt in the Assembly Bomb Case
June 8, 1929

(Read in the Court on 6th June, 1929, by Mr. Asaf Ali on behalf of Bhagat Singh and B.K. Dutt)

We stand charged with certain serious offences, and at this stage it is but right that we must explain our conduct.

In this connection, the following questions arise.

1. Were the bombs thrown into Chamber, and, if so, why?
2. Is the charge, as framed by the Lower Court, correct or otherwise?

To the first half of first question, our reply is in the affirmative, but since some of the so-called 'eye witnesses' have perjured themselves and since we are not denying our liability to that extent, let our statement about them be judged for what it is worth. By way of an illustration, we many point out that the evidence of Sergeant Terry regarding the seizure of the pistol from one of us is a deliberate falsehood, for neither of us had the pistol at the time we gave ourselves up. Other witnesses, too, who have deposed to having seen bombs being thrown by us have not scrupled to tell lies. This fact had its own moral for those who aim at judicial purity and fair play. At the same time, we acknowledge the fairness of the Public Prosecutor and the judicial attitude of the Court so far.

Viceroy's Views Endorsed

In our reply to the next half of the first question, we are constrained to go into some detail to offer a full and frank explanation of our motive and the circumstances leading up to what has now become a historic event.

When we were told by some of the police officers, who visited us in jail that Lord Irwin in his address to the joint session of the two houses described the event as an attack directed against no individual but against an institution itself, we readily recognized that the true significance of the incident had been correctly appreciated. We are next to none in our love for humanity. Far from having any malice against any individual, we hold human life sacred beyond words. We are neither perpetrators of dastardly outrages, and, therefore, a disgrace to the country, as the pseudo-socialist Dewan. Chaman Lal is reported to have described us, nor are we 'Lunatics' as The Tribune of Lahore and some others would have it believed.

Practical Protest

We humbly claim to be no more than serious students of the history and conditions of our country and her aspirations. We despise hypocrisy, Our practical protest was against the institution, which since its birth, has eminently helped to display not only its worthlessness but its far-reaching power for mischief.

They more we have been convinced that it exists only to demonstrate to world Indian's humiliation and helplessness, and it symbolizes the overriding domination of an irresponsible and autocratic rule. Time and again the national demand has been pressed by the people's representatives only to find the waste paper basket as its final destination.

Attack on Institution

Solemn resolutions passed by the House have been contemptuously trampled underfoot on the floor of the so called Indian Parliament. Resolution regarding the repeal of the repressive and arbitrary measures have been treated with sublime contempt, and the government measures and proposals, rejected as unacceptable buy the elected members of the legislatures, have been restored by mere stroke of the pen. In short, we have utterly failed to find any justification for the existence of an institution which, despite all its pomp and splendour, organized with the hard earned money of the sweating millions of India, is only a hollow show and a mischievous make-believe. Alike, have we failed to comprehend the mentality of the public leaders who help the Government to squander public time and money on such a manifestly stage-managed exhibition of Indian's helpless subjection.

No Hope for Labour

We have been ruminating upon all these matters, as also upon the wholesale arrests of the leaders of the labour movement. When the introduction of the Trade Disputes Bill brought us into the Assembly to watch its progress, the course of the debate only served to confirm our conviction that the labouring millions of India had nothing to expect from an institution that stood as a menacing monument to the strangling of the exploiters and the serfdom of the helpless labourers.

Finally, the insult of what we consider, an inhuman and barbarous measure was hurled on the devoted head of the representatives of the entire country, and the starving and struggling millions were deprived of their primary right and the sole means of improving their economic welfare. None who has felt like us for the dumb driven drudges of labourers could possibly witness this spectacle with equanimity. None whose heart bleeds for them, who have given their life-blood in silence to the building up of the economic structure could repress the cry which this ruthless blow had wrung out of our hearts.

Bomb Needed

Consequently, bearing in mind the words of the late Mr. S.R. Das, once Law Member of the Governor – General's Executive Council, which appeared in the famous letter he had addressed to his son, to the effect that the 'Bomb was necessary to awaken England from her dreams', we dropped the bomb on the floor of the Assembly Chamber to register our protest on behalf of those who had no other means left to give expression to their heart-rending agony. Our sole purpose was "to make the deaf hear" and to give the heedless a timely warning. Others have as keenly felt as we have done, and from under the seeming stillness of the sea of Indian humanity, a veritable storm is about to break out. We have only hoisted the "danger-signal" to warn those who are speeding along without heeding the grave dangers ahead. We have only marked the end of an era of Utopian non-violence, of whose futility the rising generation has been convinced beyond the shadow of doubt.

Ideal Explained

We have used the expression Utopian non-violence, in the foregoing paragraph which requires some explanation. Force when aggressively applied is "violence" and is, therefore, morally unjustifiable, but when it is used in the furtherance of a legitimate cause, it has its moral justification. The elimination of force at all costs in Utopian, and the mew movement which has arisen in the country, and of that dawn we have given a warning, is inspired by the ideal which guided Guru Gobind Singh and Shivaji, Kamal Pasha and Riza Khan, Washington and Garibaldi, Lafayette and Lenin.

As both the alien Government and the Indian public leaders appeared to have shut their eyes to the existence of this movement, we felt it as our duty to sound a warning where it could not go unheard. We have so far dealt with the motive behind the incident in question, and now we must define the extent of our intention.

No Personal Grudge

We bore no personal grudge or malice against anyone of those who received slight injuries or against any other person in the Assembly. On the contrary, we repeat that we hold human life sacred beyond words, and would sooner lay down our own lives in the service of humanity than injure anyone else. Unlike the mercenary soldiers of the imperialist armies who are disciplined to kill without compunction, we respect, and, in so far as it lies in our power, we attempt to save human life. And still we admit having deliberately thrown the bombs into the Assembly Chamber. Facts however, speak for themselves and our intention would be judged from the result of the action without bringing in Utopian hypothetical circumstances and presumptions.

No Miracle

Despite the evidence of the Government Expert, the bombs that were thrown in the Assembly Chamber resulted in slight damage to an empty bench and some slight abrasions in less than half a dozen cases, while Government scientists and experts have ascribed this result to a miracle, we see nothing but a precisely scientific process in all this incident. Firstly, the two bombs exploded in vacant spaces within the wooden barriers of the desks and benches, secondly, even those who were within 2 feet of the explosion, for instance, Mr. P. Rau, Mr. Shanker Rao and Sir George Schuster were either not hurt or only slightly scratched. Bombs of the capacity deposed to by the Government Expert (though his estimate, being imaginary is exaggerated), loaded with an effective charge of potassium chlorate and sensitive (explosive) picrate would have smashed the barriers and laid many low within some yards of the explosion.

Again, had they been loaded with some other high explosive, with a charge of destructive pellets or darts, they would have sufficed to wipe out a majority of the Members of the Legislative Assembly. Still again we could have flung them into the official box which was occupied by some notable persons. And finally we could have ambushed Sir John Simon whose luckless Commission was loathed by all responsible people and who was sitting in the President's gallery at the time. All these things, however, were beyond our intention and bombs did no more than they were designed to do, and the miracle consisted in no more than the deliberate aim which landed them in safe places.

We then deliberately offered ourselves to bear the penalty for what we had done and to let the imperialist exploiters know that by crushing individuals, they cannot kill ideas. By crushing two insignificant units, a nation cannot be crushed. We wanted to emphasize the historical lesson that *lettres de cachets* and Bastilles could not crush the revolutionary movement in France. Gallows and the Siberian mines could not extinguish the Russian Revolution. Bloody Sunday, and Black and Tans failed to strangle the movement of Irish freedom. Can ordinances and Safety Bills snuff out the flames of freedom in India? Conspiracy cases, trumped up or discovered and the incarceration of all young men, who cherish the vision of a great idea, cannot check the march of revolution. But a timely warning, if not unheeded, can help to prevent loss of life and general sufferings. We took it upon ourselves to provide this warning and our duty is done.

(Bhagat Singh was asked in the lower court what he meant by word "Revolution". In answer to that question, he said:) "Revolution" does not necessarily involve sanguinary strife nor is there any place in it for individual vendetta. It is not the cult of the bomb and the pistol. By "Revolution" we mean that the present order of things, which is based on manifest injustice, must change. Producers or labourers in spite of being the most necessary element of society, are robbed by their exploiters of the fruits of their labour and deprived of their elementary rights. The peasant who grows corn for all, starves with his family, the weaver who supplies the world market with textile fabrics, has not enough to cover his own and his children's bodies, masons, smiths and carpenters who raise magnificent palaces, live like pariahs in the slums. The capitalists and exploiters, the parasites of society, squander millions on their whims. These terrible inequalities and forced disparity of chances are bound to lead to chaos. This state of affairs cannot last long, and it is obvious, that the present order of society in merry-making is on the brink of a volcano.

The whole edifice of this civilization, if not saved in time, shall crumble. A radical change, therefore, is necessary and it is the duty of those who realize it to reorganize society on the socialistic basis. Unless this thing is done and the exploitation of man by man and of nations by nations is brought to an end, sufferings and carnage with which humanity is threatened today cannot be prevented. All talk of ending war and ushering in an era of universal peace is undisguised hypocrisy.

By "Revolution", we mean the ultimate establishment of an order of society which may not be threatened by such breakdown, and in which the sovereignty of the proletariat should be recognized and a world federation should redeem humanity from the bondage of capitalism and misery of imperial wars.

This is our ideal, and with this ideology as our inspiration, we have given a fair and loud enough warning.

If, however, it goes unheeded and the present system of Government continues to be an impediment in the way of the natural forces that are swelling up, a grim struggle will ensure involving the overthrow of all obstacles, and the establishment of the dictatorship of the dictatorship of the proletariat to pave the way for the consummation of the ideal of revolution. Revolution is an inalienable right of mankind. Freedom is an imperishable birth right of all. Labour is the real sustainer of society. The sovereignty of the ultimate destiny of the workers.

For these ideals, and for this faith, we shall welcome any suffering to which we may be condemned. At the altar of this revolution we have brought our youth as an incense, for no sacrifice is too great for so magnificent a cause. We are content, we await the advent of Revolution.

"Long Live Revolution."

Hunger-Strikers' Demands

June 24, 1929

[Bhagat Singh and B.K. Dutt were sentenced to transportation for life in the Delhi Assembly Bomb Case. After conviction they were transferred to Mianwali and Lahore jails respectively. They started hunger strike for better treatment to political prisoners in jails. After a few days Bhagat Singh was also shifted from Mianwali to Lahore Central Prison. Dutt was already there. They jointly addressed this letter to the Home Member, Government of India, enumerating their demands. From here started a period of prolonged struggle for better treatment to political prisoners in jails.]

Central Jail
Lahore
24.6.29

WE, BHAGAT SINGH AND B. K. DUTT, WERE SENTENCED to life transportation in the Assembly Bomb Case, Delhi the 19th April, 1929. As long as we were under trial prisoners in Delhi Jail, we were accorded a very good treatment from that jail to the Mianwali and Lahore Central Jails respectively, we wrote an application to the higher authorities asking for better diet and a few other facilities, and refused to take the jail diet.

Our demands were as follows:

We, as political prisoners, should be given better diet and the standard of our diet should at least be the same as that of European prisoners. (It is not the sameness of dietary that we demand, but the sameness of standard of diet.)

We shall not be forced to do any hard and undignified lobours at all.

All books, other than those proscribed, along with writing materials, should be allowed to us without any restriction.

At least one standard daily paper should be supplied to every political prisoner.

Political prisoners should have a special ward of their own in every jail, provided with all necessities as those of the Europeans. And all the political prisoners in one jail must be kept together in that ward.

Toilet necessities should be supplied.

Better clothing.

We have explained above the demands that we made. They are the most reasonable demands. The Jail authorities told us one day that the higher authorities have refused to comply with our demands.

Apart from that, they handle us very roughly while feeding us artificially, and Bhagat Singh was lying quite senseless on the 10th June, 1929, for about 15 minutes, after the forcible feeding, which we request to be stopped without any further delay.

In addition, we may be permitted to refer to the recommendations made in the U.P. Jail Committee by Pt. Jagat Narain and K.B. Hafiz Hidayat Hussain. They have recommended the political prisoners to be treated as "Better Class Prisoners."

We request you to kindly consider our demands at your earliest convenience.

By "Political Prisoners", we mean all those people who are convicted for offences against the State, for instance the people who were convicted in the Lahore Conspiracy Cases, 1915-17, the Kakori Conspiracy Cases and Sedition Cases in general.

Yours

Bhagat Singh

B. K. Dutt

Letter to I.G. (Prisons), Punjab Mianwali Jail

June 17, 1929

[Prelude to a prolonged struggle in jail on the demand of a better treatment.]

17 June, 1929

To
The Inspector-General (Jails),
Punjab Jails

Dear Sir,

Despite the fact that I will be prosecuted along with other young men arrested in Saunders shooting case, I have been shifted to Mianwali Jail from Delhi. The hearing of the case is to start from 26 June, 1929. I am totally unable to understand the logic behind this kind of shifting. Whatever it be, justice demands that every under trial should be given all those facilities which help him to prepare and contest the case. How can I appoint any lawyer while I am here? It is difficult to keep on the contact with my father and other relatives. This place is quite isolated, the route is troublesome and it is very far from Lahore.

I request you that you order my immediate transfer to Lahore Central Jail so that I get an opportunity to prepare my case. I hope that it will be given the earliest consideration.

Yours truly
Bhagat Singh

Message to Punjab Students' Conference

October 19, 1929

[The Second Punjab Students' Conference was held at Lahore on October 19, 1929, under the persidentship of Subhash Chandra Bose. Bhagat Singh grabbed the opportunity and sent this message asking the students to plunge whole-heartedly into the coming movement of 1930-31 and carry the message of revolution to the remotest corners of the country. It was jointly signed with B. K. Dutt. The message was read in the open session. It received a thunderous applause from the students with the slogans of Bhagat Singh Zindabad!]

COMRADES

Today, we cannot ask the youth to take to pistols and bombs. Today, students are confronted with a far more important assignment. In the coming Lahore Session the Congress is to give call for a fierce fight for the independence of the country. The youth will have to bear a great burden in this difficult times in the history of the nation. It is true that students have faced death at the forward positions of the struggle for independence. Will they hesitate this time in proving their same staunchness and self-confidence? The youth will have to spread this revolutionary message to the far corner of the country. They have to awaken crores of slum-dwellers of the industrial areas and villagers living in worn-out cottages, so that we will be independent and the exploitation of man by man will become an impossibility. Punjab is considered politically backward even otherwise. This is also the responsibility of the youth. Taking inspiration from the martyr Yatindra Nath Das and with boundless reverence for the country, they must prove that they can fight with steadfast resolve in this struggle for independence.

On the Slogan of 'Long Live Revolution'[6]

December 24, 1929

To,

The Editor Modern Review

You have in the December (1929) issue of your esteemed magazine, written a note under the caption "Long Live Revolution" and have pointed out the meaninglessness of this phrase. It would be impertinent on our part to try to refute or contradict the statement of such an old, experienced and renowned journalist as your noble self, for whom every enlightened Indian has profound admiration. Still we feel it our duty to explain what we desire to convey by the said phrase, as in a way it fell to our lot to give these "cries" a publicity in this country at this stage.

We are not the originators of this cry. The same cry had been used in Russian revolutionary movement. Upton Sinclair, the well

6. Shri Ramanand Chaterji the editor of *Modern Review,* ridiculed the slogan of 'Long Live Revolution' through an editorial note and gave an entirely wrong interpretation. Bhagat Singh wrote a reply and handed it over to the trying magistrate to be sent to *Modern Review.* This was published in *The Tribune* of December 24, 1929.

known socialist writer, has, in his recent novels *Boston* and *Oil,* used this cry through some of the anarchist revolutionary characters. The phrase never means that the sanguinary strife should ever continue, or that nothing should ever be stationary even for a short while. By long usage this cry achieves a significance which may not be quite justifiable from the grammatical or the etymological point of view, but nevertheless we cannot abstract from that the association of ideas connected with that. All such shouts denote a general sense which is partly acquired and partly inherent in them. For instance, when we shout "Long Live Jatin Das", we cannot and do not mean thereby that Das should physically be alive. What we mean by that shout is that the noble ideal of his life, the indomitable spirit which enabled that great martyr to bear such untold suffering and to make the extreme sacrifice for that we may show the same unfailing courage in pursuance of our ideal. It is that spirit that we allude to.

Similarly, one should not interpret the word "Revolution" in its literal sense. Various meanings and significances are attributed to this word, according to the interests of those who use or misuse it. For the established agencies of exploitation it conjures up a feeling of blood stained horror. To the revolutionaries it is a sacred phrase. We tried to clear in our statement before the Session Judge, Delhi, in our trial in the Assembly Bomb Case, what we mean by the word "Revolution"

We stated therein that Revolution did not necessarily involve sanguinary strife. It was not a cult of bomb and pistol. They may sometimes be mere means for its achievement. No doubt they play a prominent part in some movements, but they do not – for that very reason – become one and the same thing. A rebellion is not a revolution. It may ultimately lead to that end. The sense in which the word Revolution is used in that phrase, is the spirit, the longing for a change for the better. The people generally get accustomed to the established order of things and begin to tremble at the very idea of a change. It is this lethargical spirit that needs be replaced by the revolutionary spirit. Otherwise degeneration gains the upper hand and the whole humanity is led stray by the reactionary forces. Such a state of affairs leads to stagnation and paralysis in human progress. The spirit of Revolution should always permeate the soul of humanity, so that the reactionary forces may not accumulate (strength) to check its eternal onward march. Old order should change, always and ever, yielding place to new, so that one "good" order may not corrupt the world. It is in this sense that we raise the shout "Long Live Revolution"

Yours sincerely,
Bhagat Singh
B. K. Dutt

Statement before the Lahore High Court Bench[7]

1930

[Through this brilliant statement Bhagat Singh demolished the basis of the Sessions Court judgment and emphasized the importance of motive. The motive of action, he argued, should be the main consideration while judging the offence of an accused.]

My Lords,

We are neither lawyers nor masters of English language, nor holders of degrees. Therefore, please do not expect any oratorial speech from us. We therefore pray that instead of going into the language mistakes of our statement Your Lordships will try to understand the real sense of it.

Leaving other points to our lawyers, I will confine myself to one point only. The point is very important in this case. The point is as to what were our intentions sand to what extent we are guilty. This is a very complicated question and no one will be able to express before you that height to mental elevation which

7. The original English text could not be traced; Hindi and Urdu translation, however, are handy. We therefore re-translated it from Hindi.

inspired us to think and act in a particular manner. We want that this should be kept in mind while assessing our intentions our offence. According to the famous jurist Solomon, one should not be punished for his criminal offence if his aim is not against law.

We had submitted a written statement in the Sessions Court. That statement explains our aim and, as such, explains our intentions also. But the leaned judge dismissed it with one stroke of pen, saying that "generally the operation of law is not affected by how or why one committed the offence. In this country the aim of the offence is very rarely mentioned in legal commentaries."

My Lords, our contention is that under the circumstances the learned judge ought to have judged us either by the result of our action or on the basis of the psychological part of our statement. But he did not take any of these factors into consideration.

The point to be considered is that the two bombs we threw in the Assembly did not harm anybody physically or economically. As such the punishment awarded to us is not only very harsh but revengeful also. Moreover, the motive knowing his psychology. And no one can do justice to anybody without taking his motive into consideration. If we ignore the motive, the biggest general of the words will appear like ordinary murderers; revenue officers will look like thieves and cheats. Even judges will be accused of murder. This way the entire social system and the civilization will be reduced to murders, thefts and cheating. If we ignore the motive, the government will have no right to expect sacrifice from its people and its officials. Ignore the motive and every religious preacher will be dubbed as a preacher of falsehoods, and every prophet will be charged of misguiding crores of simple and ignorant people.

If we set aside the motive, then Jessus Christ will appear to be a man responsible for creating disturbances, breaking peace and preaching revolt, and will be considered to be a "dangerous personality" in the language of the law. But we worship him. He commands great respect in our hearts and his image creates vibrations of spiritualism amongst us. Why? Because the inspiration behind his actions was that of a high ideal. The rulers of that age could not recognize that high idealism. They only saw his outward actions. Nineteen centuries have passed since then. Have we not progressed during this period? Shall we repeat that mistake again? It that be so, then we shall have to admit that all the sacrifices of the mankind and all the efforts of the great martyrs were useless and it would appear as if we are still at the same place where we stood twenty centuries back.

From the legal point of view also, the question of motive is of special importance. Take the example of General Dyer. He resorted to firing and killed hundreds of innocent and unarmed people. But the military court did not order him to be shot. It gave him lakhs of rupees as award. Take another example. Shri Kharag Bahadur Singh, a young Gurkha, Killed a Marwari in Calcutta. If the motive be set aside, then Kharag Bahadur Singh ought to have been hanged. But he was awarded a mild sentence of a few years only. He was even released much before the expiry of his sentence. Was there any loophole in the law that he escaped capital punishment? Or, was the charge of murder not proved against him? Like us, he also accepted the full responsibility of his action, but he escaped death. He is free today. I ask Your Lordship, why was he not awarded capital punishment? His action was well calculated and well planned. From the motive end, his action was more serious and fatal than ours. He was awarded a mild punishment because his intentions were good. He was awarded a mild punishment because his intention were good. He saved the society from a dirty leach who had sucked the life-blood of so many pretty young girls. Kharag Singh was given a mild punishment just to uphold the formalities of the law.

This principle (that the law does not take motive into consideration – ed.) is quite absurd. This is against the basic principles of the law which declares that "the law is for man and not man for the law". As such, why the same norms are not being applied to us also? It is quite clear that while convicting Kharag Singh his motive was kept in mind, otherwise a murderer can never escape the hangman's noose. Are we being deprived of the ordinary advantage of the law because our offence is against the government, or because our action has a political importance?

My Lords, under these circumstances, please permit us to assert that a government which seeks shelter behind such mean methods has no right to exist. If it is exists, it is for the time being only, and that too with the blood of thousands of people on its head. If the law does not see the motive there can be no justice, nor can there be stable peace.

Mixing of arsenic (poison) in the flour will not be considered to be a crime, provided its purpose is to kill rats. But if the purpose is to kill a man, it becomes a crime of murder. Therefore, such laws which do not stand the test of reason and which are against the principle of justice, should be abolished. Because of such unjust laws, many great intellectuals had to adopt the path of revolt.

The facts regarding our case are very simple. We threw two bombs in the legislative Assembly on April 8, 1929. As a result of the explosion, a few persons received minor scratches. There was pandemonium in the chamber, hundreds of visitors and members of the Assembly ran out. Only my friend B.K. Dutt and myself remained seated in the visitors' gallery and offered ourselves for arrest. We were tried for attempt to murder, and convicted for life.

As mentioned above, as a result of the bomb explosion, only four or five persons were slightly injured and one bench got damaged. We offered ourselves for arrest without any resistance. The Sessions Judge admitted that we could have very easily escaped, had we had any intention like that. We accepted our offence and gave a statement explaining our position. We are not afraid of punishment. But we do not want that we should be wrongly understood. The judge remover a few paragraphs from our statement. This we consider to be harmful for our real position.

A proper study of the full text of our statement will make it clear that, according to us, our country is passing through a delicate phase. We saw the coming catastrophe and thought it proper to give a timely warning with a loud voice, and we gave the warning in the manner we thought proper. We may be wrong. Our line of thinking and that of the learned judge may be different, but that does not mean that we be deprived of the permission to express our ideas, and wrong things be propagated in our name.

In our statement we explained in detail what we mean by "Long Live Revolution" and "Down With Imperialism". That formed the crux of our ideas. That portion was removed from our statement. Generally a wrong meaning is attributed to the word revolution. That is not our understanding. Bombs and pistols do not make revolution. That is not our understanding. Bombs and pistols do not make revolution. The sword of revolution is sharpened on the whetting-stone of ideas. This is what we wanted to emphasize. By revolution we mean the end of the miseries of capitalist wars. It was not proper to pronounce judgment without understanding our aims and objects and the process of achieving them. To associate wrong ideas with our names is out and out injustice.

It was very necessary to give the timely warning that the unrest of the people is increasing and that the malady may take a serious turn, if not treated in time and properly. If our warning is not heeded, no human power will be able to stop it. We took this step to give proper direction to the storm. We are serious students of history. We believe that, had the ruling powers acted correctly at the proper time, there would have been no bloody revolutions in France and Russia. Several big power of the world tried to check the storm of ideas and were sunk in the atmosphere of bloodshed. The ruling people cannot change the flow of the current. We wanted to give the first warning. Had we aimed at killing some important personalities, we would have failed in the attainment of our aim.

My Lords, this was the aim and the spirit behind our action, and the result of the action corroborates our statement. There is one more point which needs elucidation, and that is regarding the strength of the bombs. Had we had no idea of the strength of the bombs, there would have been no question of our throwing them in the presence of our respected national leader like Pandit Motilal Nehru, Shri Kelkar, Shri Jayaker and Shri Jinnah. How could we have risked the lives of our leaders? After all we are not mad and, had we been so, we would have certainly been sent to the lunatic asylum, instead of being put in jail. We had full knowledge about the strength of the bombs and that is why we acted with so much confidence. It was very easy to have thrown the bombs on the occupied benches, but it was difficult to have thrown them on unoccupied seats. Had we not of saner mind or had we been mentally unbalanced, the bombs would have fallen on occupied benches and not in empty places. Therefore I would say that we should be rewarded for the courage we showed in carefully selecting the empty places. Under these conditions, My Lords, we think we have not been understood, My Lords, we think we have not been understood properly. We have not come before you to get our sentences reduced. We have come here to clarify our position. We want that we should not be given any unjust treatment, nor should any unjust opinion be pronounced about us. The question of punishment is of secondary importance before us.

Regarding Suicide

Letter to Sukhdev, 1930

[Hearing of the case was over. Judgment was expected any day. Sukhdev expected life transportation for him. To him the idea of remaining in jail for 20 years was repulsive. He wrote to Bhagat Singh that in case he (Sukhdev) is convicted for life he will commit suicide. He stood for release or death; no middle course. Bhagat Singh's reaction to Sukhdev's letter was very sharp. Serve, suffer and live to struggle for the cause – that was his stand. "Escaping from hardships is cowardice", he said. This letter provides one more window to peep into the martyr's mind.]

Dear Brother,

I have gone through your letter attentively and many times. I realize that the changed situation has affected us differently. The things you hated outside have now become essential to you. In the same way, the things I used to support strongly are of no significance to me anymore. For example, I believed in personal love, but now this feeling has ceased to occupy any particular position in my heart and mind. While outside, you were strongly opposed to it but now a drastic change and radicalization is apparent in your ideas about it. You experience it as an extremely essential part of human existence and you have found a particular kind of happiness in the experience.

You may still recollect that one day I had discussed suicide with you. That time I told you that in some situations suicide may be justifiable, but you contested my point. I vividly remember the time and place of our conversation. We talked about this in the Shahanshahi Kutia one evening. You said in jest that such a cowardly act can never be justified. You said that acts of this kind were horrible and heinous, but I see that you have now made an about-turn on this subject. Now you find it not only proper in certain situations but also necessary, even essential. My opinion is what you had held earlier, that suicide is a heinous crime. It is an act of complete cowardice. Leave alone revolutionaries, no individual can ever justify such an act.

You say you fail to understand how suffering alone can serve the country. Such a question from a person like you is really perplexing, because how much thoughtfully we loved the motto of the Naujawan Bharat Sabha – "to suffer and sacrifice through service". I believe that you served as much as was possible. Now is the time when you should suffer for what you did. Another point is that this is exactly the moment when you have to lead the entire people.

Man acts only when he is sure of the justness of his action, as we threw the bomb in the Legislative Assembly. After the action, it is the time for bearing the consequences of that act. Do you think that had we tried to avoid the punishment by pleading for mercy, we would have been more justified? No, this would have had an adverse effect on the masses. We are now quite successful in our endeavour.

At the time of our imprisonment, the condition for the political prisoners of our party were very miserable. We tried to improve that. I well you quite seriously that we believed we would die very shortly. Neither we were aware of the technique of forced feeding nor did we ever think of it. We were ready to die. Do you mean to say that we were intending to commit suicide? No. Striving and sacrificing one's life for a superior ideal can never be called suicide. We are envious of the death of our Comrade Yatindra Nath Das. Will you call it suicide? Ultimately, our sufferings bore fruit. A big movement started in the whole of the country. We were successful in our aim. Death in the struggles of this kind is an ideal death.

Apart from this, the comrades among us, who believe that they will be awarded death, should await that day patiently when the sentence will be announced and they will be hanged. This death will also be beautiful, but committing suicide – to cut short the life just to avoid some pain – is cowardice. I want to tell you that obstacles make a man perfect. Neither you nor I, rather none of us, have suffered any pain so far. That part of our life has started only now.

You will recollect that we have talked several times about realism in the Rusian literature, which is nowhere visible in our own. We highly appreciate the situations of pain in their stories, but we do not feel that spirit of suffering within ourselves. We also admire their passion and the extraordinary height of their characters, but we never bother to find out the reason. I will say that only the reference to their resolve to bear pain has produced the intensity, the suffering of pain, and this has given great depth and height to their characters and literature. We become pitiable and ridiculous when we imbibe an unreasoned mysticism in our life without any natural or substantial basis. People like us, who are proud to be revolutionary in every sense, should always be prepared to bear all the difficulties, anxieties, pain and suffering which we invite upon ourselves by the struggles initiated by us and for which we call ourselves revolutionary.

I want to tell you that in jail, and in jail alone, can a person get an occasion to study empirically the great social subjects of crime and sin. I have read some literature on this and only the jail is the proper place for the self-study on all these topics. The best parts of the self-study for one is to suffer oneself.

You know it that the suffering of political prisoners in the jails of Russia caused, in the main, the revolution in the prison-administration after the overthrow of Czardom. Is India not in need of such persons who are fully aware of this problem and have personal experience of these things? It will not suffice to say that someone else would do it, or that many other people are there to do it. Thus, men who find it quite dishonourable and hateful to leave the revolutionary responsibilities to others should start their struggle against the existing system with total devotion. They should violate these rules but they should also keep in mind the propriety, because unnecessary and improper attempts can never be considered just. Such agitations will shorten the process of revolution. All the arguments which you gave to keep yourself aloof from all such movement, are incomprehensible to me. Some of our friends are either fools or ignorant. They find your behaviour quite strange and incomprehensible. (They themselves say they cannot comprehend it because you are above and very far from their understanding.)

In fact, if you feel that jail life is really humiliating, why don't you try to improve it by agitating? Perhaps, you will say that this struggle would be futile, but this is precisely the argument which is usually used as a cover by weak people to avoid participation in every movement. This is the reply which we kept on hearing outside the jail from the people who were anxious to escape from getting entangled in revolutionary movements. Shall I now hear the same argument from you? What could our party of a handful of people do in comparison to the vastness of its aims and ideals? Shall we infer from this that we erred gravely in starting our work altogether? No, inferences of this kind will be improper. This only shows the inner weakness of the man who thinks like this.

You write further that it cannot be expected of a man that he will have the same thinking after going through 14 long years of suffering in the prison, which he had before, because the jail life will crush all his ideas. May I ask you whether the situation outside the jail was any bit more favourable to our ideas? Even then, could we have left it because of our failures? Do you mean to imply that had we not entered the field, no revolutionary work would have taken place at all? If this be your contention, then you are mistaken, though it is right that we also proved helpful to an extent in changing the environment. But, the, we are only a product of the need of our times.

I shall even say that Marx – the father of communism – did not actually originate this idea. The Industrial Revolution of Europe itself produced men of this kind. Marx was one among them. Of course, Marx was also instrumental to an extent in gearing up the wheels of his time in a particular way.

I (and you too) did not give birth to the ideas of socialism and communism in this country; this is the consequence of the effects of our time and situations upon ourselves. Of course, we did a bit to propagate these ideas, and therefore I say that since we have already taken a tough task upon ourselves, we should continue to advance it. The people will not be guided by our committing suicides to escape the difficulties; on the contrary, this will be quite a reactionary step.

We continued our work despite the testing environment of disappointments, pressures and violence ordained by the jail rules. While we worked, we were made target of many kinds of difficulties. Even men who were proud to proclaim themselves to be great revolutionaries, deserted us. Were these conditions not testing in the extreme? Then, what was the reason and the logic of continuing our agitation and efforts?

Does this simple argument not by itself give added strength to our ideas? And, don't we have instances of our revolutionary comrades who suffered for their convictions in jails and are still working on return from jails? Had Bakunin argued like you, he would have committed suicide right in the beginning. Today, you find many revolutionaries occupying responsible posts in the Russian state who had passed the greater part of their lives in prison, completing their sentences. Man must try hard to stick to his beliefs. No one can say what future has in store.

Do you remember that when we were discussing that some concentrated and effective poison should also be kept in our bomb factories, you opposed it very vehemently. The very idea was repugnant to you. You had no faith in it. So, what has happened now? Here, even the difficult and complex conditions do not obtain. I feel revulsion even in discussing this question. You hated even that attitude of mind which permits suicide. You will kindly excuse me for saying that had you acted according to this belie right at the time of your imprisonment (that is, you had committed suicide by taking poison), you would have served the revolutionary cause, but at this moment, even the thought of such an act is harmful to our cause.

There is just one more point which I will like to draw your attention to. We do not believe in God, hell and heaven, punishment and rewards, that is in any Godly accounting of human life. Therefore, we must think of life and death on materialist lines. When I was brought here from Delhi for the purpose of identification, some intelligence officers talked to me on this topic, in the presence of my father. They said that since I did not try to save of my life by divulging secrets, it proved the presence of an acute agony in my life. They argued that a death of this kind will be something like suicide. But I had replied that a man with beliefs and ideal like mine, could never think of dying uselessly. We want to get the maximum value for our lives. We want to serve humanity as much as possible. Particularly a man like me, whose life is nowhere sad or worried, can never think of suicide even, leave alone attempting it. The same thing I want to tell you now.

I hope you will permit me to tell you what I think about myself. I am certain of capital punishment for me. I do not expect even a bit of moderation or amnesty. Even if there is amnesty, it will not be for all, and even that amnesty will be for other only, not for us; it will be extremely restricted and burdened with various conditions. For, us neither there can be any amnesty nor it will ever happen. Even then, I wish that release calls for us should be made collection and globally. Along with that, I also wish that when the movement reaches its climax, we should be hanged. It is my wish that if at any time any honourable and fair compromise is possible, issue like our case may never obstruct it. When the fate of the country is being decided, the fate of individuals should be forgotten. As revolutionaries, we do not believe that there can be any sudden change in the attitude of our rulers, particularly in the British race. Such a surprising change is impossible without through sustained striving, sufferings and sacrifices. And it shall be achieved. As far as my attitude is concerned, I can welcome facilities and amnesty for all only when its effect is permanent and some indelible impressions are made on the hearts of the people of the country through our hanging. Only this much and nothing more.

Reasons for Refusing to Attend the Court

January, 1930

[The second hunger strike of the LCC accused was also suspended after twenty-one days on the assurance given by the government. But there were so many minor issues and complaints which the magistrate was not prepared to listen to. The accused thereupon refused to attend the court. The Civil and Military Gazette (an Anglo-Indian daily from Lahore) commented that the accused had boycotted the British court. This was wrong. Bhagat Singh contradicted it and explained the reasons for refusing to attend the court.]

Mister Magistrate

After going through your order dated 4 February, 1930, which was published in The Civil and Military Gazette, it appears necessary that we explain to you the reason of our boycott of the court.

It is wrong to say that we have boycotted the courts of the British government. Today, we are going to the court of Mr. Louis who is hearing the case initiated against us under Section 22 of the Jail Act. We had presented our problems and difficulties in our bail application before you, but it still remains unconsidered.

Our comrades under trial belong to different and distant corner of the country. Therefore, they should be given the facility of meeting their well wishers and sympathizers. Shri B.K. Dutt gave an application to meet Miss Lajjawati, and Shri Kamal Nath Tewari also wanted to meet someone, but were neither their relatives nor their lawyers. Even after securing their authorization, they were not allowed to meet. It is quite clear from this that the under trials are not given the facilities for their defense. Not merely this, Comrade Kranti Kumar, who was doing very useful work for our defense committee and was also providing us with things of daily use, has been imprisoned on a fabricated charge. It has come to our knowledge that when the fabricated charge of bringing bullets in the sauce, could not be proved against him, under Section 124 A in Gurudaspur which is distant from Lahore.

I myself cannot keep a whole time lawyer: therefore I wanted that my trusted friends should observe the court proceedings by being present there, but they were denied permission without any explicit reason, and only Lala Amardas, Advocate, has been given a seat.

We can never like this drama acted in the name of justice, because we do not get any facility or benefit for defending ourselves. One more serious complaint is against non-available of newspapers. Under trial prisoners cannot be treated like convicted prisoners. We should be given at least one newspaper regularly. We want one newspaper also for those who do not know English. Therefore, as a protest, we are returning even the English. Therefore, as a protest, we are returning even the English daily Tribune. We decided to boycott the court on 29 January, 1930, because of these complaints. We will rejoin the proceedings when these inconveniences are removed.

Yours

etc. etc.

Telegram on Lenin's Death Anniversary

January 21, 1930

[On January 21, 1930, the accused in the Lahore Conspiracy Case appeared in the court wearing red scarves. As soon as the magistrate took his chair they raised slogans "Long Live Socialist Revolution", "Long Live Communist International", "Long Live People" "Lenin's Name Will Never Die", and "Down with Imperialism". Bhagat Singh then read the text of this telegram in the court and asked the magistrate to send it to the Third International.]

ON LENIN DAY WE SEND HEARTY GREETINGS TO ALL who are doing something for carrying forward the ideas of the great Lenin. We wish success to the great experiment Russia is carrying out. We join our voice to that of the international working class movement. The proletariat will win. Capitalism will be defeated. Death to Imperialism.

Hunger-Strikers' Demands Reiterated

January 28, 1930

[The Lahore Conspiracy Case (LCC) prisoners had suspended their hunger strike on the assurance that the Government of India was considering the Jail Committee Report and that the jail reforms would be punished for participating in the hunger strike. After the hunger strike was suspended, the GOI, however, resorted to delaying tactics. Disciplinary acting was also taken against hunger strikers in U.P. and Punjab jails (other than LCC prisoners). It was in this connection that Bhagat Singh wrote this letter to the GOI, which was short of a notice-cum-ultimatum for resuming the hunger strike.]

The Home Member,
The Govt. of India
Delhi

Through
The Special Magistrate,

Lahore Conspiracy Case,
Lahore

Sir,
With reference to our telegram dated 20th Jan. 1930, reading as follows, we have not been given any reply.

Home Member Government. Delhi Under trials, Lahore Conspiracy Case and other Political Prisoners suspended hunger-strike on the assurance that the India Govt. was considering Provincial Jail Committee's reports. All Government Conference over. No action yet taken. As vindictive treatment to political prisoners still continues, we request we be informed within a week final Govt. decision. Lahore Conspiracy Case under trials.

As briefly stated in the above telegram, we beg to bring to your kind notice that the Lahore Conspiracy Case under trials and several other political prisoners confined in Punjab jails suspended hunger strike on the assurance given by the members of the Punjab Jail Enquiry Committee that the question of the treatment of political prisoners was going to be finally settled to our satisfaction within a very short period. Further, after the death of our great martyr Jatindra Nath Das, the matter was taken up in the Legislative Assembly and the same assurance was given publicly by Sir James Crerar. It was then pronounced that there has been a change of heart and the question of the treatment of political prisoners was receiving the utmost sympathy of the government. Such political prisoners who were still on hunger strike in jails of the different parts of the country then suspended their hunger strike on the request being made to this effect in an AICC resolution passed in view of the said assurance and the critical condition of some of the prisoners.

Since then all the local governments have submitted their reports. A meeting of Inspectors- General of Prisons of different provinces has been held at Lucknow and the deliberations of the All-India Govt. Conference have been concluded at Delhi. The All-India Conference was held in the month of Dec. last. Over not carried into effect any final recommendations. By such dilatory attitude of the government we no less than the general public have begun to fear that perhaps the question has been shelved. Our apprehensions have been strengthened by the vindictive treatment meted out to hunger strikers and other political prisoners during the last four months. It is very difficult for us to know the details of the hardships to which the political prisoners are being subjected. Still the little information that has trickled out of the four walls of the jails in sufficient to furnish us with glaring instances. We give below a few such instances which we cannot but feel, are not in conformity with the govt. assurance.

(1) Sj. B.K. Banerji, undergoing 5 years imprisonment in connection with Dakshineshwar Bomb Case in Lahore Central Jail, joined the hunger strike last year. Now as a punishment for the same, for each day of his period of hunger strike, two days of the remission so far earned by him have been forfeited. Under usual circumstances his release was due in Dec. last, but it will be delayed by full four months. In the same Jail similar punishment has been awarded to Baba Sohan Singh, an old man of about seventy, now undergoing his sentence of life transportation in connection with the (first) Lahore Conspiracy Case. Besides, among others, Sardar Gopal Singh confined in Mianwali Jail, Master Mota Singh confined in Rawalpindi Jail have also been awarded vindictive punishments for joining the general hunger strike. In most of these cases

the periods of imprisonment have been enhanced while some of them have been removed from the Special class.

(2) For the same offence, i.e. joining the general hunger strike, Messrs. Sachindra Nath Sanyal, Ram Kishan Khattri and Suresh Chandra Bhattacharya, confined in Agra Central Jail, Raj Kumar Sinha, Sachindra Nath Bukshi, Manmath Nath Gupta and several other Kakori case prisoners have been severely punished. It is reliably learnt that Mr. Sanyal was given bar-fetters and solitary cell-confinement and as a consequence there has been a break-down in his health. His weight has gone down by eighteen pounds. Mr. Bhattacharya is reported to be suffering from tuberculosis. The three Bareilly Jail prisoners also have been punished. It is learnt that all their privileges have been withdrawn. Even their usual rights of interviewing with relations and communication with them were forfeited. They have all been considerably reduced in their weights. Two press statements have been issued in this connection in Sep. 1929 and Jan. 1930 by Pandit Jawaharlal Nehru.

(3) After the passing of the AICC resolution regarding hunger strike, the copies of the same, which were sent to different political prisoners, were withheld by the jail authorities. Further, the govt. refused a Congress deputation to meet the prisoners in this respect.

(4) The Lahore Conspiracy Case under trials were assaulted brutally on 23rd and 24th Oct., 1929, by orders of high police officials. Full details have appeared in the press. The copy of the statement of the one of us recorded by the Special Magistrate, Pt. Shri Krishan, has been duly forwarded to you in a communication dated 16th Dec.,

1929 Neither the Punjab Government nor the Govt. of India felt it necessary to reply or even acknowledge receipt of our communication praying for an enquiry. While, on the other hand, local government has felt the imperative necessity of prosecuting us in connection with the very same incident for offering "violent" resistance".

(5) In the last week of Dec. 1929, Sj. Kiran Chandra Das and eight others confined in the Lahore Borstal Jail, when being taken to and produced in the Magistrate's Court, were found handcuffed and chained together in flagrant breach of the unanimous recommendations of the Punjab Jail Enquiry Committee and also of Inspector-General of Prisons, Punjab. It is further noteworthy that these prisoners were under trials, changed for a bailable offence. A long statement issued by Dr. Mohd. Aslam, Lala Duni Chand of Lahore and Lala Duni Chand of Ambala in this connection was published in Tribune.

When we learnt these and other sufferings of the political prisoners we refrained from resuming our hunger strike, though we were much grieved as we thought that the matter was going to be finally settled at an early date, but in the light of the above instances, are we now to believe that the untold sufferings of the hunger strikers and the supreme sacrifice made by Jatin Das have all been in vain? Are we to understand that the govt. gave its assurance only to check the growing tide of public agitation and to avert a crisis? You will agree with us if we say that we have waited patiently for a sufficiently reasonable period of time. But we cannot wait indefinitely. The government, buy its dilatory attitude and the continuation of vindictive treatment to political prisoners, has left us no other option but to resume the struggle. We realize that to go on hunger strike and to carry it on is no easy task.

But let us at the same time point out that Indiacan produce many more Jatins and Wagias, Ran Rakshas and Bhan Singhs. (The last two named laid down their lives in the Andamans in 1917 – the first breathed his last after 63 days of hunger strike while the other died the death of a great hero after silently undergoing in human tortures for full six months.)

Enough has been said by us and the members of the public (inquiry committee) in justification of the better treatment of political prisoners and it is unnecessary here to repeat the same. We would however like to say a few words as regards the inclusion of motive as the basis and the most important factor in the matter of classification. Great fuss has been created on the question of criteria of classification. We find that motive has altogether been excluded so far from the criteria suggested by different provincial governments This is really strange attitude. It is through motive alone that the real value of any action can be decided. Are we to understand that the Government is unable to distinguish between a robber who robs and kills his victim and a Kharag Bahadur who kills a villain and saves the honour of a young lady and redeems society of a most licentious parasite? Are both to be treated as two men belonging to the same category? Is there no difference between two men who commit the same offence, one guided buy selfish motive and the other by a selfless one? Similarly, is there no difference between a common murderer and a political worker, even if the latter resorts to violence? Does not his selflessness elevate his place from amongst those of ordinary criminals? In these circumstances we think that motive should be held as the most important factor in the criteria for classification.

Last year, in the beginning of our hunger strike, when public leaders including Dr. Gopi Chand and Lala Duni Chand of Ambala – the last named being one of the signatories to the Punjab

Jail Enquiry Committee Report – approached us to discuss the same thing and when they told us that the government considered to treat the political prisoners convicted of offences of violent nature as Special class prisoners, then by way of compromise we agreed to the proposal to the extent of excluding those actually charged with murder. But, Later on, the discussion took a different turn and the communiqué containing the terms of reference for the Punjab Jail Enquiry Committee was so worded that the question of motive seemed to be altogether excluded, and the classification was based on two thing:

(1) Nature of Offence; and

(2) Social Status of "Offender".

These criteria, instead of solving the problem, made it all the more complicated.

We could understand two classes amongst the political prisoners, those charged for non-violent offences and those charged for violent offences. But then creeps in the question of social status in the report of the Punjab Jail Enquiry Committee. As Chaudhary Afzal Haque has pointed out, and rightly too, in his note of dissent to this report, what will be the fate of those political workers who have been reduced to pauper's conditions due to their honorary services in the cause of freedom? Are they to be left at the mercy of a magistrate who will away try to prove the bonafide of his loyalty by classifying everyone as an ordinary convict? Or, is it expected that a non-cooperator will stretch his hand before the people against whom he is fighting as an opponent, begging for better treatment in jail? Is this the way of removing the causes of dissatisfaction, or rather intensifying them? It might be argued that people living in property outside the jails, should not expect luxuries inside the prison when they are detained for the purpose of punishment. But, are the reforms that are demanded, of a nature of luxury? Are they not the bare necessities of life, according to the most moderate standard of living? Inspite of all the facilities that can possibly be demanded, jail will ever remain a jail. The prison in itself does not contain and can never contain any magnetic power to attract the people from outside. Nobody will commit offences simply to come to jail. Moreover, may we venture to say that it is a very poor argument on the part of any government to say that its citizens have been driven to such extreme destitution that their standard of living has fallen even lower than that of jails? Does not such an argument cut at the very root of that government's right of existence? Anyhow, we are not concerned with that at present. What we want to say is that the best way to remove the prevailing dissatisfaction would be to classify the political prisoners as such into a separate class which may further be subdivided, if need be, into two classes – one for those convicted of nonviolent offences and the other for persons whose offences include violence. In that case motive will become one of the deciding factors. To say that motive cannot be ascertained in political cases is hypocritical assertion. What is it that today informs the jail authorities to deprive the 'political' even of the ordinary privileges? What it is that deprives them of the special grades or 'nambardaries', etc.? What does make the authorities to keep them aloof and separated from all other convicts? The same thing can help in the classification also.

As for the special demands, we have already stated them in full in our memorandum to the Punjab Jail Enquiry Committee. We would however particularly emphasize that no political prisoner, whatever his offence may be, should be given any hard and undignified labour for which he may not feel aptitude. All of them, confined in one jail, should be kept together in the same ward. At least one standard daily newspaper in vernacular or English should be given to them. Full and proper facilities for study should be granted. Lastly, they should be allowed to supplement their expenses for diet and clothing from their private sources.

We still hope that the government will carry into effect without further delay its promise made to us and to the public, so that there may not be another occasion for resuming the hunger strike. Unless and until we find a definite move on the part of the government to redeem its promise in the course of the next seven days, we shall be forced to resume the hunger strike.

Yours, etc.
Bhagat Singh, Dutt
Others
dated: 28th Jan., 1930
Under trials, Lahore Conspiracy Case

Regarding the LCC Ordinance

May 2, 1930

[The strategy of the LCC accused was to prolong the case and use the court as a platform for propagating the aims and objects of the revolutionary party. The government saw the game, and to expedite the proceedings, withdrew the case from the lower court, and promulgated an ordinance known as the LCC Ordinance No. 3 of 1930. Equipped with the Ordinance, it appointed a Special Tribunal of three High Court judges, handed over the case to it, empowered it to dispense with the witnesses and proceed with the case even in the absence of the accused. The Governor-Genera, while justifying the step, said that the accused were resorting to hunger strikes again and again and were making it impossible for the court to proceed. It was in this context that Bhagat Singh wrote this letter to the Governor – General to demolish his argument.]

To
His Excellency
The Governor-General of India
Simla,
2nd May, 1930

Sir,

The full text of the special Ordinance to expedite our trial has been read over to us. To Tribunal has also been appointed by the Chief Justice of the Punjab High Court of Juridicature. We welcome the news. We could have kept silent, had you not referred to our attitude adopted so far in this case, and thus tried to throw the sole responsibility on our shoulders. In the present situation, we feel it necessary to make a statement to clear our position.

We have been marking from the very beginning that the Govt. authorities have always been trying to deliberately misrepresent us. After all, this is a fight, and the misrepresentation is and has always been the best instrument in the hands of the Govt. to meet their enemies. We have absolutely no grudge against this mean tactic. However, there are certain things the consideration of which is forcing us to make the following counter.

You have mentioned your statement issued along with the Lahore Conspiracy Ordinance, our hunger strike. As you have yourself admitted, two of us had begun the hunger strike weeks before the commencement of the inquiry into this case in the court of R.S Pt. Sri Krishan, Special Magistrate. Hence any man with the least common sense can understand that the hunger strike had nothing to do with the trial. The Govt. had to admit the existence of these grievances. When the Govt. made some gesture as to making certain arrangement for the settlement of this question, and Provincial Jail Enquiry Committees were appointed for the same purpose, we gave up the hunger strike. But at first we were informed that the question would be finally settled in November. Then it was postponed till December. But January also passed and there was not the least to indicate as to whether the Govt. was going to the do anything in this connection at all, or not. We feared that the matter was shelved. Hence the second hunger strike on 4th Feb., 1930, after full one week's notice. It was only then that the Govt. tried to settle this question finally. A Communiqué was published and we again gave up the hunger strike and did not even wait to see the final decision, in this connection, carried into effect. It is only today that we are realizing that the British Govt. has not yet given u the policy of telling lies even in such ordinary matters as this. This Communiqué is in specific terms, but we find something quite contrary in practice. Anyhow, this is not the proper place to discuss that question; we might have to deal with it later on, if the occasion arises. But what we want to emphasize here is that the hunger strike was never directed against the proceedings of the court. Such great sufferings cannot be invited and such great sacrifice cannot be made with that ordinary motive. Das did not lay down his life for such a trivial cause. Rajguru and others did not risk their lives simply to protract the trial.

You know thoroughly well, and everybody concerned knows it, that it is note hunger strike that has forced you to promulgate this Ordinance. There is something else the consideration of which confused the heads of your Government it is neither the protraction of the case nor any other emergency which forces you to sign this lawless law. It is certainly some-thing different.

But let us declare once and for all that our spirits cannot be cowed down by ordinances. You may crush certain individuals but you cannot crush this nation. As far as this Ordinance is concerned, we consider it to be our victory. We had been from the very beginning pointing out that this existing law was a mere make – believe. It could not administer justice. But even those privileges to which the accused were legitimately and legally entitled and which are given to ordinary accused were legitimately and legally entitled and which are given to ordinary accused, could not be given to the accused in political cases. We wanted to make the Govt. throw off its veil and to be candid enough to admit that fair chances for defense could not be given to the political accused. Here we have the frank admission of the Government. We congratulate you as well as your Govt. for this candour and welcome the Ordinance.

Insipte of the frank admission of your agents, the Special Magistrate and the Prosecution Counsels, as to the reasonableness of our attitude throughout, you had been confused at the very thought of the existence of our case. What else is needed to assure us of our success in this fight.

Statement of the Undefended Accused

May 5, 1930

[For propaganda purposes the LCC accused had divided themselves into three groups. The first group consisted of comrades who were represented through a lawyer. This was a small group of comrades against whom there was not much evidence and who had chances of getting acquitted.

The second group consisted of the unrepresented accused. Bhagat Singh belonged to this group. Comrades of this group were generally vocal in the court. They cross-examined the prosecution witnesses, challenged the prosecution, challenge the rulings of the court, delivered political speeches, and made every effort to prolong the proceedings.

The third group consisted of the undefended accused. They were to challenge the bonafides of the court and the government. It consisted of five comrades. On the very first day they submitted a written statement before the Tribunal, saying that they did not recognise the alien government and the court appointed by it, and that they did not expect any justice from the enemy court. The statement was prepared by Bhagat Singh and was read in the court by Jitendra Nath Sanyal. The other four signatories were Mahabir Singh, Gaya Prashad Kaitiyar, Kundal Lal and Batukeshwar Dutt. The Tribunal declared it as seditious, banned it and refused to record it as part of the proceedings.]

To:

The Commissioner,

The Special Tribunal

Lahore Conspiracy Case, Lahore.

Sirs,

On behalf of the five of my comrades, including myself, I feel it necessary to make the following statement at the very commencement of the trial and wish that it be retained on the record.

We do not propose to take any part in the proceedings of this case because we do not recognise this Govt. which is said to be based on justice or established by law.

We believe and do hereby declare that

"Man being the source of all the authority, no individual or govt. can be entitled to any authority unless and until it is directly derived from the people."

Since this Govt. is an utter negative of these principles, its very existence is not justifiable. Such govts. Which are organized to exploit the oppressed nations, have no right to exist except by the right of the sword (i.e., brute force) with which they try to curb all the ideas of liberty and freedom and the legitimate aspirations of the people.

We believe all such govts., and particularly this British Govt. thrust upon the helpless but unwilling Indian nation, to be no better than an organized gang of robbers, and a pack of exploiters equipped with all the means of carnage and devastation. In the name of "law and order", they crush all those who dare to expose or oppose them.

We believe that imperialism is nothing but a vast conspiracy organized with predatory motives. Imperialism is the last stage of development of insidious exploitation of man by man and of nation by nation. The imperialists, with a view to further their piratical designs, not only commit judicial murders through their law courts but also organize general massacres, devastations and other horrible crimes like war. They feel no hesitation in shooting down innocent and unarmed people who refuse to yield to their depredatory demands or to acquiesce in their ruinous and abominable designs. Under the garb of custodians of 'law and order', they break peace, create disorder, kill people and commit all conceivable crimes.

We believe that freedom is an undeniable birth-right of all people, that every man has the inalienable right of enjoying the fruits of his labour, and that every nation is indisputably the master of its resources. If any govt. deprives them of these primary rights, it is the right of the people – nay, it is their duty – to destroy that govt. Since the British Govt. is a negation of these principles for which we stand, it is our firm conviction that every effort made, every method adopted to bring about a revolution and to destroy this Govt. is morally justified. We stand for a change, a radical change in the existing order of affairs in social, political and economic spheres, and the complete replacement of the existing order by a new one rendering the exploitation of man by man impossible and thus guaranteeing full liberty to all the people in all the spheres. We feel that unless the whole social order is changed and socialistic society is established, the whole world is in danger of a disastrous catastrophe.

As regards the methods, peaceful or otherwise, to be adopted for the consummation of the revolutionary ideal, let us declare that the choice rests with those who hold power. Revolutionaries, by virtue of their altruistic principles, are lovers of peace – a genuine and permanent peace based on justice and equality, not the illusory peace resulting from cowardice and maintained at the point of bayonets. If the revolutionaries take to bombs and pistols, it is only as a measure of terrible necessity, as a last recourse.

We believe that "Law and Order is for man and not man for Law and Order."

As the supreme jurlis [SIC; Original transcription is unclear – MIA transcriber] council of Revolutionary France has well expressed:

"The end of law is not to abolish or restrain but to preserve and enlarge freedom. The legitimate power is required to govern by promulgated laws established for the common good alone and resting ultimately on the consent and the authority of the people, from which law no one is exempted – not even the legislators."

The sanctity of law can be maintained only so long as it is the expression of the will of the people. When it becomes a mere instrument in the hands of an oppressing class, it loses its sanctity and significance, for the fundamental preliminary condition for administration of justice is the elimination of every interest. As soon as the law ceases to correspond to the popular social needs, it becomes the means for perpetration of injustice and tyranny. The maintaining of such a law is nothing but a hypocritical assertion of a special interest against the common interest.

The law of the present Govt. exist for the interest of the alien rulers, against the interest of our people, and as such they have no moral binding whatsoever. It is therefore incumbent duty of all Indians of defy and disobey these laws. The British law courts, as part and parcel of the machinery of exploitation, cannot administer justice – especially in political cases where there is a clash between the interests of the Govt. and the people. We know that these courts are nothing but the stages for the performance of mockery of justice.

For these reasons we decline to be a party to this farcical show and, henceforth, we shall not take any part in the proceedings of this case.

Yours,
J.N. Sanyal,
B.K. Dutt,
Dr. Gayal Prasad,
Kundan Lal
May 5, 1930

Letter to Jaidev Gupta

July 24, 1930

[Bhagat Singh wrote this letter to Jaidev Gupta, a close friend from his schools days, for some books. It gives an idea of the type of books he used to study in jail. It also shows as to how keen he was about the intellectual development of his comrades.]

Lahore Central Jail
24.7.30

My Dear Jaidev,

Please take following books in my name from Dwarkadas Library and send them through Kulvir on Sunday:

Militarism (Kari Liebknecht) Why Men Fight (B. Russel)
Soviets at Work Collapse of the Second International
Left-Wing Communism Mutual Aid (Prince Kropotkin)
Fields, Factories and Workshops Civil War in France (Marx)
Land Revolution in Russia Spy (Upton Sinclair)

Please send one more book from Punjab Public Library: Historical Materialism (Bukharin). Also, please find out from the librarian if some books have been sent to Borstal Jail. They are facing a terrible famine of books. They had sent a list of books through Sukhdev's brother Jaidev. They have not received any book till now. In case they have no list, then please ask Lala Firoz Chand to send some interesting books of his choice. The books must reach them before I go there on this Sunday. This work is a must. Please keep this in mind.

Also send Punjab Peasants in Prosperity and Debt by Darling and 2 or 3 books of this type for Dr. Alam. Hope you will excuse me for this trouble. I promise I will not trouble you in future. Please remember me to all my friends and convey my respect to Lajjawati. I am sure if Dutt's sister came she will not forget to see me.

With regards
Bhagat Singh

Justice Hilton Must also Go

June 25, 1930

[Our case before the Special Tribunal opened on May 5, 1930. On May 12 the presiding judge lost his temper on the question of a song. He ordered that the accused be handcuffed. The accused resisted. They were removed from the court by force and sent back to the jails. The accused boycotted the court from the next day onward and demanded that the presiding judge must apologize, on he should be removed.

On June 21 the presiding judge was removed, but along with him the Government removed Justice Agha Haider also who was the next senior judge and was sympathetic towards the accused.

On June 23 the accused went to the court to find Justice Hilton, who was a party to the order, presiding over the Tribunal. The accused objected to it and demanded that either Justice Hilton should dissociate himself from the order or he should apologize, failing which he should also dissociate himself from the order or he should apologize, failing which he should also be removed from the Tribunal. It was in this context that Bhagat Singh wrote this letter.]

To
The Commissioner,
The Special Tribunal,Lahore Conspiracy Case,
Lahore

Sir,

Whereas two judges of the Tribunal have withdrawn or have been made to withdraw themselves from the Tribunal and two new judges have been appointed in their place, we feel that a statement is very necessary on our part to explain our position clearly so that no misunderstanding may be possible.

It was on 12th May, 1930, that an order was passed by Mr. Justice Cold stream, the then President, to handcuff us in asking the court to inform us as to the cause of this sudden and extraordinary order was not thought worth consideration. The police handcuffed us forcibly and removed us back to jail. One of the three judges, Mr. Agha Harider, on the following day, dissociated himself with that order of the President. Since that day we have not been attending court.

Our condition on which we were prepared to attend court was laid before the Tribunal on the next day, namely that either the President should apologize or he should be replaced; by this we never meant that a judge who was a party to that order should take the place of the President.

For more than five weeks no heed was paid to the grievances of the accused.

According to the present formation of the Tribunal, both the President and the other judge who had dissociated himself from the order of the President, have been replaced by two new judges. Thus the judge who was a party to that order – as the President gave the order on behalf of the majority – has now been appointed the President of the Tribunal. In these circumstances we want to emphasize one thing that we had absolutely no grudge against the person of Mr. Justice Cold stream. We had protested against the order passed by the President on behalf of the majority and the subsequent maltreatment meted out to us. We have every respect for Mr. Justice Cold stream and Mr. Justice Hilton that should be expected from man to man. And as our protest was against a certain order we wanted the President to apologize, which meant apology by the President on behalf of the Tribunal who was responsible for that order. By the removal of the President the Position is not changed because Mr. Justice Hilton, who was a party to the order, is presiding in place position has added an insult to injury.

Yours, etc.

Bhagat Singh, B.K. Dutt

25th June, 1930

Letter to Father

October 4, 1930

[When the case was in its final stage, Sardar Kishan Singh (Bhagat Singh's father) made a written request to the Tribunal, saying that there were many facts to prove that his son was innocent and that he had nothing to do with Sounder's murder. He also requested that his son be given an opportunity to prove his innocence. When Bhagat Singh came to know of it he was very angry, and wrote this strong letter to his father, protesting against his move.]

Oct. 4, 1930

My Dear Father,

I was astounded to learn that you had submitted a petition to the members of the Special Tribunal in connection with my defence. This intelligence proved to be too severe a blow to be borne with equanimity. It has upset the whole equilibrium of my mind. I have not been able to understand how you could think it proper to submit such a petition at this stage and in these circumstances. Inspite of all the sentiments and feelings of a father, I don't think you were at all entitled to make such a move on my behalf without even consulting me. You know that in the political field my views have always differed with those of yours. I have always been acting independently without having cared for your approval or disapproval.

I hope you can recall to yourself that since the very beginning you have been trying to convince me to fight my case very seriously and to defend myself properly. But you also know that I was always opposed to it. I never had any desire to defend myself and never did I seriously think about it. Whether it was a mere vague ideology or that I had certain arguments to justify my position, is a different question and that cannot be discussed here.

You know that we have been pursuing a definite policy in this trial. Every action of mine ought to have been consistent with that policy, my principle and my programme. At present the circumstances are altogether different, but had the situation been otherwise, even then I would have been the last man to offer defence. I had only one idea before me throughout the trial, i.e. to show complete indifference towards the trial inspite of serious nature of the charges against us. I have always been of opinion that all the political workers should be indifferent and should never bother about the legal fight in the law courts and should boldly bear the heaviest possible sentences inflicted upon them. They may defend themselves but always from purely political considerations and never from a personal point of view. Our policy in this trial has always been consistent with this principle; whether we were successful in that or not is not for me to judge. We have always been doing our duty quite disinterstedly.

In the statement accompanying the text of Lahore Conspiracy Case Ordinance the Viceroy had stated that the accused in this case were trying to bring both law and justice into contempt. The situation afforded us an opportunity to show to the public whether we are trying to bring law into contempt or whether others were doing so. People might disagree with us on this point.

You might be one of them. But that never meant that such moves should be made on my behalf without my consent or even my knowledge. My life is not so precious, at least to me, as you may probably think it to be. It is not at all worth buying at the cost of my principles. There are other comrades of mine whose case is as serious as that of mine. We had adopted a common policy and we shall stand to the last, no matter how dearly we have to pay individually for it.

Father, I am quite perplexed. I fear I might overlook the ordinary principle of etiquette and my language may become a little but harsh while criticizing or rather censoring this move on your part. Let me be candid. I feel as though I have been stabbed at the back. Had any other person done it, I would have considered it to be nothing short o treachery. But in your case, let me say that it has been a weakness – a weakness of the worst type.

This was the time where everybody's mettle was being tested. Let me say, father, you have failed. I know you are as sincere a patriot as one can be. I know you are as sincere a patriot as one can be. I know you have devoted your life to the cause of Indian independence, but why, at this moment, have you displayed such a weakness? I cannot understand.

In the end, I would like to inform you and my other friends and all the people interested in my case, that I have not approved of your move. I am still not at all in favour of offering any defence. Even if the court had accepted that petition submitted by some of my co-accused regarding defence, etc., I would have not defended myself. My applications submitted to the Tribunal regarding my interview during the hunger strike, were misinterpreted and it was published in the press that I was going to offer defence, though in reality I was never willing to offer any defence. I still hold the same opinion as before. My friends in the Borstal Jail will be taking it as a treachery and betrayal on my part. I shall not even get an opportunity to clear my position before them.

I want that public should know all the details about this complication, and, therefore, I request you to publish this letter.

Your loving son

Bhagat Singh

Why I am an Atheist

October 5 - 6, 1930

It is a matter of debate whether my lack of belief in the existence of an Omnipresent, Omniscient God is due to my arrogant pride and vanity. It never occurred to me that sometime in the future I would be involved in polemics of this kind. As a result of some discussions with my friends, (if my claim to friendship is not uncalled for) I have realised that after having known me for a little time only, some of them have reached a kind of hasty conclusion about me that my atheism is my foolishness and that it is the outcome of my vanity. Even then it is a serious problem. I do not boast of being above these human follies. I am, after all, a human being and nothing more. And no one can claim to be more than that. I have a weakness in my personality, for pride is one of the human traits that I do possess. I am known as a dictator among my friends. Sometimes I am called a boaster. Some have always been complaining that I am bossy and I force others to accept my opinion. Yes, it is true to some extent. I do not deny this charge. We can use the word 'vainglory' for it. As far as the contemptible, obsolete, rotten values of our society are concerned, I am an extreme sceptic. But this question does not concern my person alone. It is being proud of my ideas, my thoughts. It cannot be called empty pride. Pride, or you may use the word, vanity, both mean an exaggerated assessment of one's personality. Is my atheism because of unnecessary pride, or have I ceased believing in God after thinking long and deep on the matter? I wish to put my ideas before you. First of all, let us differentiate between pride and vanity as these are two different things.

I have never been able to understand how unfounded, baseless pride or empty vanity can hinder a person from believing in God. I may refuse to acknowledge the greatness of a really great person only when I have got fame without doing any serious efforts or when I lack the superior mental powers necessary to become great. It is easy to understand but how is it possible that a believer can turn into a non-believer because of his vanity? Only two things are possible: either a man deems himself to be in possession of Godly qualities, or he goes a step further and declares himself to be a god. In both these states of mind he cannot be an atheist in the true sense of the word. In the first case, it is not an outright rejection of God's existence; in the other, he is affirming the existence of some kind of supernatural power responsible for the working of universe. It does not harm our argument whether he claims to be a god or considers God to be a reality in existence above his own being. The real point, however, is that in both cases he is a theist, a believer. He is not an atheist. I want to bring home this point to you. I am not one of these two creeds. I totally reject the existence of an Omnipresent, all powerful, all knowing God. Why so? I will discuss it later in the essay. Here I wish to emphasise that I am not an atheist for the reason that I am arrogant or proud or vain; nor am I a demi-god, nor a prophet; no, nor am I God myself. At least one thing is true that I have not evolved this thought because of vanity or pride. In order to answer this question I relate the truth. My friends say that after Delhi bombing and Lahore Conspiracy Case,

I rocketed to fame and that this fact has turned my head. Let us discuss why this allegation is incorrect. I did not give up my belief in God after these incidents. I was an atheist even when I was an unknown figure. At least a college student cannot cherish any sort of exaggerated notion of himself that may lead him to atheism. It is true that I was a favourite with some college teachers, but others did not like me. I was never a hardworking or studious boy. I never got an opportunity to be proud. I was very careful in my behaviour and somewhat pessimistic about my future career. I was not completely atheistic in my beliefs. I was brought up under the care and protection of my father. He was a staunch Arya Samaji. An Arya Samaji can be anything but never an atheist. After my elementary education, I was sent to D. A. V College, Lahore. I lived in the boarding house for one year. Besides prayers early in the morning and at dusk time, I sat for hours and chanted religious Mantras. At that time, I was a staunch believer. Then I lived with my father. He was a tolerant man in his religious views. It is due to his teachings that I devoted my life for the cause of liberating my country. But he was not an atheist. His God was an all-pervading Entity. He advised me to offer my prayers every day. In this way I was brought up. In the Non-cooperation days, I got admission to the National College. During my stay in this college, I began thinking over all the religious polemics such that I grew sceptical about the existence of God. In spite of this fact I can say that my belief in God was firm and strong. I grew a beard and 'Kais' (long head of hair as a Sikh religious custom). In spite of this I could not convince myself of the efficacy of Sikh religion or *any religion at all, for that matter*. But I had an unswerving, unwavering belief in God.

Then I joined the Revolutionary Party. The first leader I met had not the courage to openly declare himself an atheist. He was unable to reach any conclusion on this point. Whenever I asked him about the existence of God, he gave me this reply: "You may believe in him when you feel like it." The second leader with whom I came in contact was a firm believer. I should mention his name. It was our respected Comrade Sachindara Nath Sanyal. He was sentenced to life imprisonment in connection with Karachi conspiracy case. Right from the first page of his only book, 'Bandi Jivan' (Incarnated Life) he sings praises to the Glory of God. See the last page of the second part of this book and you find praises showered upon God in the way of a mystic. It is a clear reflection of his thoughts.

According to the prosecution, the 'Revolutionary Leaflet' which was distributed throughout India was the outcome of Sachindara Nath Sanyal's intellectual labour. So often it happens that in revolutionary activities a leader expresses his own ideas which may be very dear to him, but in spite of having differences, the other workers have to acquiesce in them.

In that leaflet, one full paragraph was devoted to the praises of God and His doings which we, human beings, cannot understand. This is sheer mysticism. What I want to point out is that the idea of denying the existence of God did not even occur to the Revolutionary Party. The famous Kakory martyrs, all four of them, passed their last day in prayers. Ram Parshad Bismal was a staunch Arya Samaji. In spite of his vast studies in Socialism and Communism, Rajan Lahiri could not suppress his desire to recite hymns from Upanishads and Gita. There was but only one person among them who did not indulge in such activities. He used to say, "Religion is the outcome of human weakness or the limitation of human knowledge." He is also in prison for life. But he also never dared to deny the existence of God.

Till that time I was only a romantic revolutionary, just a follower of our leaders. Then came the time to shoulder the whole responsibility. For some time, a strong opposition put the very existence of the party into danger. Many leaders as well as many enthusiastic comrades began to uphold the party to ridicule. They jeered at us. I had an apprehension that someday I will also consider it a futile and hopeless task. It was a turning point in my revolutionary career. An incessant desire to study filled my heart. 'Study more and more', said I to myself so that I might be able to face the arguments of my opponents. 'Study' to support your point of view with convincing arguments. And I began to study in a serious manner. My previous beliefs and convictions underwent a radical change. The romance of militancy dominated our predecessors; now serious ideas ousted this way of thinking. No more mysticism! No more blind faith! Now realism was our mode of thinking. At times of terrible necessity, we can resort to extreme methods, but violence produces opposite results in mass movements. I have talked much about our methods. The most important thing was a clear conception of our ideology for which we were waging a long struggle. As there was no election activity going on, I got ample opportunity to study various ideas propounded by various writers. I studied Bakunin, the anarchist leader. I read a few books of Marx, the father of Communism. I also read Lenin and Trotsky and many other writers who successfully carried out revolutions in their countries. All of them were atheists. The ideas contained in Bakunin's 'God and State' seem inconclusive, but it is an interesting book. After that I came across a book 'Common Sense' by Nirlamba Swami. His point of view was a sort of mystical atheism. I developed more interest in this subject. By the end of 1926, I was convinced that the belief in an Almighty, Supreme Being who created, guided and controlled the universe had no sound foundations. I began discussions on this subject with my friends. I had openly declared myself an atheist. What it meant will be discussed in the following lines.

In May 1927, I was arrested in Lahore. This arrest came as a big surprise for me. I had not the least idea that I was wanted by the police. I was passing through a garden and all of a sudden the police surrounded me. To my own surprise, I was very calm at that time. I was in full control of myself. I was taken into police custody. The next day I was taken to the Railway Police lockup where I spent a whole month. After many days' conversation with police personnel, I guessed that they had some information about my connection with the Kakori Party. I felt they had some intelligence of my other activities in the revolutionary movement. They told me that I was in Lucknow during the Kakori Party Trial so that I might devise a scheme to rescue the culprits. They also said that after the plan had been approved, we procured some bombs and by way of test, one of those bombs was thrown into a crowd on the occasion of Dussehra in 1926. They offered to release me on condition that I gave a statement on the activities of the Revolutionary Party. In this way I would be set free and even rewarded and I would not be produced as an approver in the court. I could not help laughing at their proposals. It was all humbug. People who have ideas like ours do not throw bombs at their own innocent people. One day, Mr. Newman, the then senior Superintendent of CID, came to me. After a long talk which was full of sympathetic words, he imparted to me what he considered to be sad news, that if I did not give any statement as demanded by them, they would be forced to send me up for trial for conspiracy to wage war in connection with Kakori Case and also for brutal killings in Dussehra gathering. After that he said that he had sufficient evidence to get me convicted and hanged.

I was completely innocent, but I believed that the police had sufficient power to do it if they desired it to be so. The same day some police officers persuaded me to offer my prayers to God two times regularly. I was an atheist. I thought that I would settle it to myself whether I could brag only in days of peace and happiness that I was an atheist, or in those hard times I could be steadfast in my convictions. After a long debate with myself, I reached the conclusion that I could not even pretend to be a believer nor could I offer my prayers to God. No, I never did it. It was time of trial and I would come out of it successful. These were my thoughts. Never for a moment did I desire to save my life. So I was a true atheist then and I am an atheist now. It was not an easy task to face that ordeal. Beliefs make it easier to go through hardships, even make them pleasant. Man can find a strong support in God and an encouraging consolation in His Name. If you have no belief in Him, then there is no alternative but to depend upon yourself. It is not child's play to stand firm on your feet amid storms and strong winds. In difficult times, vanity, if it remains, evaporates and man cannot find the courage to defy beliefs held in common esteem by the people. If he really revolts against such beliefs, we must conclude that it is not sheer vanity; he has some kind of extraordinary strength. This is exactly the situation now. First of all we all know what the judgement will be. It is to be pronounced in a week or so. I am going to sacrifice my life for a cause. What more consolation can there be! A God-believing Hindu may expect to be reborn a king; a Muslim or a Christian might dream of the luxuries he hopes to enjoy in paradise as a reward for his sufferings and sacrifices. What hope should I entertain? I know that will be the end when the rope is tightened round my neck and the rafters move from under my feet. To use more precise religious terminology, that will be the moment of utter annihilation.

My soul will come to nothing. If I take the courage to take the matter in the light of 'Reward', I see that a short life of struggle with no such magnificent end shall itself be my 'Reward.' That is all. Without any selfish motive of getting any reward here or in the hereafter, quite disinterestedly have I devoted my life to the cause of freedom. I could not act otherwise. The day shall usher in a new era of liberty when a large number of men and women, taking courage from the idea of serving humanity and liberating them from sufferings and distress, decide that there is no alternative before them except devoting their lives for this cause. They will wage a war against their oppressors, tyrants or exploiters, not to become kings, or to gain any reward here or in the next birth or after death in paradise; but to cast off the yoke of slavery, to establish liberty and peace they will tread this perilous, but glorious path. Can the pride they take in their noble cause be called vanity? Who is there rash enough to call it so? To him I say either he is foolish or wicked. Leave such a fellow alone for he cannot realise the depth, the emotions, the sentiment and the noble feelings that surge in that heart. His heart is dead, a mere lump of flesh, devoid of feelings. His convictions are infirm, his emotions feeble. His selfish interests have made him incapable of seeing the truth. The epithet 'vanity' is always hurled at the strength we get from our convictions.

You go against popular feelings; you criticise a hero, a great man who is generally believed to be above criticism. What happens? No one will answer your arguments in a rational way; rather you will be considered vainglorious. Its reason is mental insipidity. Merciless criticism and independent thinking are the two necessary traits of revolutionary thinking. As Mahatmaji is great, he is above criticism; as he has risen above, all that he says in the field of politics, religion, Ethics is right. You agree or not, it is binding upon you to take it as truth. This is not constructive thinking. We do not take a leap forward; we go many steps back.

Our forefathers evolved faith in some kind of Supreme Being, therefore, one who ventures to challenge the validity of that faith or denies the existence of God, shall be called a Kafir (infidel), or a renegade. Even if his arguments are so strong that it is impossible to refute them, if his spirit is so strong that he cannot be bowed down by the threats of misfortune that may befall him through the wrath of the Almighty, he shall be decried as vainglorious. Then why should we waste our time in such discussions? This question has come before the people for the first time, hence the necessity and usefulness of such long discussions.

As far as the first question is concerned, I think I have made it clear that I did not turn atheist because of vanity. Only my readers, not I, can decide whether my arguments carry weight. If I were a believer, I know in the present circumstances my life would have been easier; the burden lighter. My disbelief in God has turned all the circumstances too harsh and this situation can deteriorate further. Being a little mystical can give the circumstances a poetic turn. But I need no opiate to meet my end. I am a realistic man. I want to overpower this tendency in me with the help of Reason. I am not always successful in such attempts. But it is man's duty to try and make efforts. Success depends on chance and circumstances.

Now we come to the second question: if it is not vanity, there ought to be some sound reason for rejection of age-old belief in God. Yes, I come to this question. I think that any man who has some reasoning power always tries to understand the life and people around him with the help of this faculty. Where concrete proofs are lacking, [mystical] philosophy creeps in. As I have indicated, one of my revolutionary friends used to say that "philosophy is the outcome of human weakness." Our ancestors had the leisure to solve the mysteries of the world, its past, its present and its future, its whys and its wherefores, but having been terribly short of direct proofs, every one of them tried to solve the problem in his own way. Hence we find wide differences in the fundamentals of various religious creeds. Sometimes they take very antagonistic and conflicting forms. We find differences in Oriental and Occidental philosophies. There are differences even amongst various schools of thoughts in each hemisphere. In Asian religions, the Muslim religion is completely incompatible with the Hindu faith. In India itself, Buddhism and Jainism are sometimes quite separate from Brahmanism. Then in Brahmanism itself, we find two conflicting sects: Aarya Samaj and Snatan Dheram. Charwak is yet another independent thinker of the past ages. He challenged the Authority of God. All these faiths differ on many fundamental questions, but each of them claims to be the only true religion. This is the root of the evil. Instead of developing the ideas and experiments of ancient thinkers, thus providing ourselves with the ideological weapon for the future struggle, – lethargic, idle, fanatical as we are – we cling to orthodox religion and in this way reduce human awakening to a stagnant pool.

It is necessary for every person who stands for progress to criticise every tenet of old beliefs. Item by item he has to challenge the efficacy of old faith. He has to analyse and understand all the details. If after rigorous reasoning, one is led to believe in any theory of philosophy, his faith is appreciated. His reasoning may be mistaken and even fallacious. But there is chance that he will be corrected because Reason is the guiding principle of his life. But belief, I should say blind belief is disastrous. It deprives a man of his understanding power and makes him reactionary.

Any person who claims to be a realist has to challenge the truth of old beliefs. If faith cannot withstand the onslaught of reason, it collapses. After that his task should be to do the groundwork for new philosophy. This is the negative side. After that comes in the positive work in which some material of the olden times can be used to construct the pillars of new philosophy. As far as I am concerned, I admit that I lack sufficient study in this field. I had a great desire to study the Oriental Philosophy, but I could get ample opportunity or sufficient time to do so. But so far as I reject the old time beliefs, it is not a matter of countering belief with belief, rather I can challenge the efficacy of old beliefs with sound arguments. We believe in nature and that human progress depends on the domination of man over nature. There is no conscious power behind it. This is our philosophy.

Being atheist, I ask a few questions from theists:

1. If, as you believe there is an Almighty, Omnipresent, Omniscient God, who created the earth or universe, please let me know, first of all, as to why he created this world. This world which is full of woe and grief, and countless miseries, where not even one person lives in peace.

2. Pray, don't say it is His law. If He is bound by any law, He is not Omnipotent. Don't say it is His pleasure. Nero burnt one Rome. He killed a very limited number of people. He caused only a few tragedies, all for his morbid enjoyment. But what is his place in history? By what names do we remember him? All the disparaging epithets are hurled at him. Pages are blackened with invective diatribes condemning Nero: the tyrant, the heartless, the wicked.

One Genghis Khan killed a few thousand people to seek pleasure in it and we hate the very name. Now, how will you justify your all powerful, eternal Nero, who every day, every moment continues his pastime of killing people? How can you support his doings which surpass those of Genghis Khan in cruelty and in misery inflicted upon people? I ask why the Almighty created this world which is nothing but a living hell, a place of constant and bitter unrest. Why did he create man when he had the power not to do so? Have you any answer to these questions? You will say that it is to reward the sufferer and punish the evildoer in the hereafter. Well, well, how far will you justify a man who first of all inflicts injuries on your body and then applies soft and soothing ointment on them? How far the supporters and organizers of Gladiator bouts were justified in throwing men before half starved lions, later to be cared for and looked after well if they escaped this horrible death. That is why I ask: Was the creation of man intended to derive this kind of pleasure?

Open your eyes and see millions of people dying of hunger in slums and huts dirtier than the grim dungeons of prisons; just see the labourers patiently or say apathetically while the rich vampires suck their blood; bring to mind the wastage of human energy that will make a man with a little common sense shiver in horror. Just observe rich nations throwing their surplus produce into the sea instead of distributing it among the needy and deprived. There are palaces of kings built upon the foundations laid with human bones. Let them see all this and say "All is well in God's Kingdom." Why so? This is my question. You are silent. All right. I proceed to my next point.

You, the Hindus, would say: Whosoever undergoes sufferings in this life, must have been a sinner in his previous birth. It is tantamount to saying that those who are oppressors now were Godly people then, in their previous births. For this reason alone they hold power in their hands. Let me say it plainly that your ancestors were shrewd people. They were always in search of petty hoaxes to play upon people and snatch from them the power of Reason. Let us analyse how much this argument carries weight!

Those who are well versed in the philosophy of Jurisprudence relate three of four justifications for the punishment that is to be inflicted upon a wrong-doer. These are: revenge, reform, and deterrence. The Retribution Theory is now condemned by all the thinkers. Deterrent theory is on the anvil for its flaws. Reformative theory is now widely accepted and considered to be necessary for human progress. It aims at reforming the culprit and converting him into a peace-loving citizen. But what in essence is God's Punishment even if it is inflicted on a person who has really done some harm? For the sake of argument we agree for a moment that a person committed some crime in his previous birth and God punished him by changing his shape into a cow, cat, tree, or any other animal. You may enumerate the number of these variations in Godly Punishment to be at least eighty-four lack. Tell me, has this tomfoolery, perpetrated in the name of punishment, any reformative effect on human man? How many of them have you met who were donkeys in their previous births for having committed any sin? Absolutely no one of this sort! The so called theory of 'Puranas' (transmigration) is nothing but a fairy-tale. I do not have any intention to bring this unutterable trash under discussion. Do you really know the most cursed sin in this world is to be poor? Yes, poverty is a sin; it is a punishment! Cursed be the theoretician, jurist or legislator who proposes such measures as push man into the quagmire of more heinous sins. Did it not occur to your All Knowing God or he could learn the truth only after millions had undergone untold sufferings and hardships? What, according to your theory, is the fate of a person who, by no sin of his own, has been born into a family of low caste people?

He is poor so he cannot go to a school. It is his fate to be shunned and hated by those who are born into a high caste. His ignorance, his poverty, and the contempt he receives from others will harden his heart towards society. Supposing that he commits a sin, who shall bear the consequences? God, or he, or the learned people of that society? What is your view about those punishments inflicted on the people who were deliberately kept ignorant by selfish and proud Brahmans? If by chance these poor creatures heard a few words of your sacred books, Vedas, these Brahmans poured melted lead into their ears. If they committed any sin, who was to be held responsible? Who was to bear the brunt? My dear friends, these theories have been coined by the privileged classes. They try to justify the power they have usurped and the riches they have robbed with the help of such theories. Perhaps it was the writer Upton Sinclair who wrote (Bhagat Singh is referring to Sinclair's pamphlet 'Profits of Religion' – MIA transcriber) somewhere "only make a man firm believer in the immortality of soul, then rob him of all that he possesses. He will willingly help you in the process." The dirty alliance between religious preachers and possessors of power brought the boon of prisons, gallows, knouts and above all such theories for the mankind.

I ask why your Omnipotent God does not hold a man back when he is about to commit a sin or offence. It is child's play for God. Why did He not kill war lords? Why did He not obliterate the fury of war from their minds? In this way He could have saved humanity of many a great calamity and horror. Why does He not infuse humanistic sentiments into the minds of the Britishers so that they may willingly leave India? I ask why He does not fill the hearts of all capitalist classes with altruistic humanism that prompts them to give up personal possession of the means of production and this will free the whole labouring humanity from the shackles of money. You want to argue the practicability of Socialist theory, I leave it to your Almighty God to enforce it. Common people understand the merits of Socialist theory as far as general welfare is concerned but they oppose it under the pretext that it cannot be implemented. Let the Almighty step in and arrange things in a proper way. No more logic chopping! I tell you that the British rule is not there because God willed it but for the reason that we lack the will and courage to oppose it. Not that they are keeping us under subjugation with the consent of God, but it is with the force of guns and rifles, bombs and bullets, police and militia, and above all because of our apathy that they are successfully committing the most deplorable sin, that is, the exploitation of one nation by another. Where is God? What is He doing? Is He getting a diseased pleasure out of it? A Nero! A Genghis Khan! Down with Him!

Now another piece of manufactured logic! You ask me how I will explain the origin of this world and origin of man. Charles Darwin has tried to throw some light on this subject. Study his book. Also, have a look at Sohan Swami's "Commonsense." You will get a satisfactory answer. This topic is concerned with Biology and Natural History. This is a phenomenon of nature. The accidental mixture of different substances in the form of Nebulae gave birth to this earth. When? Study history to know this. The same process caused the evolution of animals and in the long run that of man. Read Darwin's 'Origin of Species.' All the later progress is due to man's constant conflict with nature and his efforts to utilise nature for his own benefit. This is the briefest sketch of this phenomenon.

Your next question will be why a child is born blind or lame even if he was not a sinner in his previous birth. This problem has been explained in a satisfactory manner by biologists as a mere biological phenomenon. According to them the whole burden rests upon the shoulders of parents whose conscious or unconscious deeds caused mutilation of the child prior to his birth.

You may thrust yet another question at me, though it is merely childish. The question is: If God does not really exist, why do people come to believe in Him? Brief and concise my answer will be. As they come to believe in ghosts, and evil spirits, so they also evolve a kind of belief in God: the only difference being that God is almost a universal phenomenon and well developed theological philosophy. However, I do disagree with radical philosophy. It attributes His origin to the ingenuity of exploiters who wanted to keep the people under their subjugation by preaching the existence of a Supreme Being; thus claimed an authority and sanction from Him for their privileged position. I do not differ on the essential point that all religions, faiths, theological philosophies, and religious creeds and all other such institutions in the long run become supporters of the tyrannical and exploiting institutions, men and classes. Rebellion against any king has always been a sin in every religion.

As regard the origin of God, my thought is that man created God in his imagination when he realized his weaknesses, limitations and shortcomings. In this way he got the courage to face all the trying circumstances and to meet all dangers that might occur in his life and also to restrain his outbursts in prosperity and affluence. God, with his whimsical laws and parental generosity was painted with variegated colours of imagination. He was used as a deterrent factor when his fury and his laws were repeatedly propagated so that man might not become a danger to society. He was the cry of the distressed soul for he was believed to stand as father and mother, sister and brother, brother and friend when in time of distress a man was left alone and helpless. He was Almighty and could do anything. The idea of God is helpful to a man in distress.

Society must fight against this belief in God as it fought against idol worship and other narrow conceptions of religion. In this way man will try to stand on his feet. Being realistic, he will have to throw his faith aside and face all adversaries with courage and valour. That is exactly my state of mind. My friends, it is not my vanity; it is my mode of thinking that has made me an atheist. I don't think that by strengthening my belief in God and by offering prayers to Him every day, (this I consider to be the most degraded act on the part of man) I can bring improvement in my situation, nor can I further deteriorate it. I have read of many atheists facing all troubles boldly, so I am trying to stand like a man with the head high and erect to the last; even on the gallows.

Let us see how steadfast I am. One of my friends asked me to pray. When informed of my atheism, he said, "When your last days come, you will begin to believe." I said, "No, dear sir, Never shall it happen. I consider it to be an act of degradation and demoralisation. For such petty selfish motives, I shall never pray." Reader and friends, is it vanity? If it is, I stand for it.

Letter to B. K. Dutt

November, 1930

[This letter gives an idea as to what Bhagat Singh expected from those comrades who would escape capital punishment.]

Central Jail,
November, 1930

Dear Brother,

The judgment has been delivered. I am condemned to death. In these cells, besides myself, there are many others prisoners who are waiting to be hanged. The only prayer of these people is that somehow or other they may escape the noose. Perhaps I am the only man amongst them who is anxiously waiting for the day when I will be fortunate enough to embrace the gallows for my ideal.

I will climb the gallows gladly and show to the world as to how bravely the revolutionaries can sacrifice themselves for the cause.

I will condemned to death, but you are sentenced to transportation for life. You will live and, while living, you will have to show to the world that the revolutionaries not only die for their ideals but can face every calamity. Death should not be a means to escape the worldly difficulties. Those revolutionaries who have by chance escaped the gallows for the ideal but also bear the worst type o tortures in the dark dingy prison cells.

Yours

Bhagat Singh

To Young Political Workers

February 2, 1931

[Written on February 2, 1931, this document is a sort of behest to young political workers of India. At that time the talk of some sort of compromise between the Congress and the British Government was in the air. Through this document Bhagat Singh explained as to when a compromise is permissible and when it is not. He also made out that the way Congress is conducting the movement it was bound to end in some sort of compromise. After analysing to the conditions then prevailing, he finally advised the youth to adopt Marxism as the ideology, work among the people, organize workers and peasants and form the Communist Party.

After Bhagat Singh's execution this document was published in a mutilated form. All references to Soviet Union, Marx, Lenin and the Communist Party were carefully deleted. Subsequently, the GOI published it in one of its secret reports in 1936. A photostat copy of the full report is preserved in the library of the Martyrs' Memorial and Freedom Struggle Research Centre at Lucknow.]

To
The Young Political Workers

Dear Comrades

Our movement is passing through a very important phase at present. After a year's fierce struggle some definite proposals regarding the constitutional reforms have been formulated by the Round Table Conference and the Congress leaders have been invited to give this [Original transcription is unclear – MIA Transcriber]... think it desirable in the present circumstances to call off their movement. Whether they decide in favour or against is a matter of little importance to us. The present movement is bound to end in some sort of compromise. The compromise may be effected sooner or later. And compromise is not such ignoble and deplorable an thing as we generally think. It is rather an indispensable factor in the political strategy. Any nation that rises against the oppressors is bound to fail in the beginning, and to gain partial reforms during the medieval period of its struggle through compromises. And it is only at the last stage – having fully organized all the forces and resources of the nation – that it can possibly strike the final blow in which it might succeed to shatter the ruler's government. But even then it might fail, which makes some sort of compromise inevitable. This can be best illustrated by the Russian example.

In 1905 a revolutionary movement broke out in Russia. All the leaders were very hopeful. Lenin had returned from the foreign countries where he had taken refuge. He was conducting the struggle. People came to tell him that a dozen landlords were killed and a score of their mansions were burnt. Lenin responded by telling them to return and to kill twelve hundred landlords and burn as many of their palaces. In his opinion that would have meant something if revolution failed. Duma was introduced. The same Lenin advocated the view of participating in the Duma.

This is what happened in 1907. In 1906 he was opposed to the participation in this first Duma which had granted more scope of work than this second one whose rights had been curtailed. This was due to the changed circumstances. Reaction was gaining the upper hand and Lenin wanted to use the floor of the Duma as a platform to discuss socialist ideas.

Again after the 1917 revolution, when the Bolsheviks were forced to sign the Brest Litovsk Treaty, everyone except Lenin was opposed to it. But Lenin said: "Peace". "Peace and again peace: peace at any cost – even at the cost of many of the Russian provinces to be yielded to German War Lord". When some anti-Bolshevik people condemned Lenin for this treaty, he declared frankly that the Bolsheviks were not in a position to face to German onslaught and they preferred the treaty to the complete annihilation of the Bolshevik Government.

The thing that I wanted to point out was that compromise is an essential weapon which has to be wielded every now and then as the struggle develops. But the thing that we must keep always before us is the idea of the movement. We must always maintain a clear notion as to the aim for the achievement of which we are fighting. That helps us to verify the success and failures of our movements and we can easily formulate the future programme. Tilak's policy, quite apart from the ideal i.e. his strategy, was the best. You are fighting to get sixteen annas from your enemy, you get only one anna. Pocket it and fight for the rest. What we note in the moderates is of their ideal. They start to achieve on anna and they can't get it. The revolutionaries must always keep in mind that they are striving for a complete revolution. Complete mastery of power in their hands. Compromises are dreaded because the conservatives try to disband the revolutionary forces after the compromise from such pitfalls. We must be very careful at such junctures to avoid any sort of confusion of the real issues especially the goal. The British Labour leaders betrayed their real struggle and have been reduced to mere hypocrite imperialists. In my opinion the diehard conservatives are better to us than these polished imperialist Labour leaders. About the tactics and strategy one should study life-work of Lenin. His definite views on the subject of compromise will be found in "Left Wing" Communism.

I have said that the present movement, i.e. the present struggle, is bound to end in some sort of compromise or complete failure.

I said that, because in my opinion, this time the real revolutionary forces have not been invited into the arena. This is a struggle dependent upon the middle class shopkeepers and a few capitalists. Both these, and particularly the latter, can never dare to risk its property or possessions in any struggle. The real revolutionary armies are in the villages and in factories, the peasantry and the labourers. But our bourgeois leaders do not and cannot dare to tackle them. The sleeping lion once awakened from its slumber shall become irresistible even after the achievement of what our leaders aim at. After his first experience with the Ahmedabad labourers in 1920 Mahatma Gandhi declared: "We must not tamper with the labourers. It is dangerous to make political use of the factory proletariat" (The Times, May 1921). Since then, they never dared to approach them. There remains the peasantry. The Bardoli resolution of 1922 clearly denies the horror the leaders felt when they saw the gigantic peasant class rising to shake off not only the domination of an alien nation but also the yoke of the landlords.

It is there that our leaders prefer a surrender to the British than to the peasantry. Leave alone Pt. Jawahar lal. Can you point out any effort to organize the peasants or the labourers? No, they will not run the risk. There they lack. That is why I say they never meant a complete revolution. Through economic and administrative pressure they hoped to get a few more reforms, a few more concessions for the Indian capitalists. That is why I say that this movement is doomed to die, may be after some sort of compromise or even without. They young workers who in all sincerity raise the cry "Long Live Revolution", are not well organized and strong enough to carry the movement themselves. As a matter of fact, even our great leaders, with the exception of perhaps Pt. Motilal Nehru, do not dare to take any responsibility on their shoulders, that is why every now and then they surrender unconditionally before Gandhi. In spite of their differences, they never oppose him seriously and the resolutions have to be carried for the Mahatma.

In these circumstances, let me warn the sincere young workers who seriously mean a revolution, that harder times are coming. Let then beware lest they should get confused or disheartened. After the experience made through two struggles of the Great Gandhi, we are in a better position to form a clear idea of our present position and the future programme.

Now allow me to state the case in the simplest manner. You cry "Long Live Revolution." Let me assume that you really mean it. According to our definition of the term, as stated in our statement in the Assembly Bomb Case, revolution means the complete overthrow of the existing social order and its replacement with the socialist order. For that purpose our immediate aim is the achievement of power. As a matter of fact, the state, the government machinery is just a weapon in the hands of the ruling class to further and safeguard its interest. We want to snatch and handle it to utilise it for the consummation of our ideal, i.e., social reconstruction on new, i.e., Marxist, basis. For this purpose we are fighting to handle the government machinery. All along we have to educate the masses and to create a favourable atmosphere for our social programme. In the struggles we can best train and educate them.

With these things clear before us, i.e., our immediate and ultimate object having been clearly put, we can now proceed with the examination of the present situation. We must always be very candid and quite business-like while analysing any situation. We know that since a hue and cry was raised about the Indians' participation in and share in the responsibility of the Indian government, the Minto-Morley Reforms were introduced, which formed the Viceroy's council with consultation rights only. During the Great War, when the Indian help was needed the most, promises about self-government were made and the existing reforms were introduced. Limited legislative powers have been entrusted to the Assembly but subject to the goodwill of the Viceroy. Now is the third stage.

Now reforms are being discussed and are to be introduced in the near future. How can our young men judge them? This is a question; I do not know by what standard are the Congress leaders going to judge them. But for us, the revolutionaries, we can have the following criteria:

1. Extent of responsibility transferred to the shoulders of the Indians.
2. From of the Government institutions that are going to be introduced and the extent of the right of participation given to the masses.
3. Future prospects and the safeguards.

These might require a little further elucidation. In the first place, we can easily judge the extent of responsibility given to our people by the control our representatives will have on the executive. Up till now, the executive was never made responsible to the Legislative

Assembly and the Viceroy had the veto power, which rendered all the efforts of the elected members futile. Thanks to the efforts of the Swaraj Party, the Viceroy was forced every now and then to use these extraordinary powers to shamelessly trample the solemn decisions of the national representatives under foot. It is already too well known to need further discussion.

Now in the first place we must see the method of the executive formation: Whether the executive is to be elected by the members of a popular assembly or is to be imposed from above as before, and further, whether it shall be responsible to the house or shall absolutely affront it as in the past?

As regards the second item, we can judge it through the scope of franchise. The property qualifications making a man eligible to vote should be altogether abolished and universal suffrage be introduced instead. Every adult, both male and female, should have the right to vote. At present we can simply see how far the franchise has been extended.

I may here make a mention about provincial autonomy. But from whatever I have heard, I can only say that the Governor imposed from above, equipped with extraordinary powers, higher and above the legislative, shall prove to be no less than a despot. Let us better call it the "provincial tyranny" instead of "autonomy." This is a strange type of democratisation of the state institutions.

The third item is quite clear. During the last two years the British politicians have been trying to undo Montague's promise for another dole of reforms to be bestowed every ten years till the British Treasury exhausts.

We can see what they have decided about the future.

Let me make it clear that we do not analyse these things to rejoice over the achievement, but to form a clear idea about our situation, so that we may enlighten the masses and prepare them for further struggle. For us, compromise never means surrender, but a step forward and some rest. That is all and nothing else.

* * *

Having discussed the present situation, let us proceed to discuss the future programme and the line of action we ought to adopt. As I have already stated, for any revolutionary party a definite programme is very essential. For, you must know that revolution means action. It means a change brought about deliberately by an organized and systematic work, as opposed to sudden and unorganised or spontaneous change or breakdown. And for the formulation of a programme, one must necessarily study:

1. The goal.
2. The premises from where were to start, i.e., the existing conditions.
3. The course of action, i.e., the means and methods.

Unless one has a clear notion about these three factors, one cannot discuss anything about programme.

We have discussed the present situation to some extent. The goal also has been slightly touched. We want a socialist revolution, the indispensable preliminary to which is the political revolution. That is what we want. The political revolution does not mean the transfer of state (or more crudely, the power) from the hands of the British to the Indian, but to those Indians who are at one with us as to the final goal, or to be more precise, the power to be transferred to the revolutionary party through popular support. After that, to proceed in right earnest is to organize the reconstruction of the whole society on the socialist basis. If you do not mean this revolution, then please have mercy. Stop shouting "Long Live Revolution." The term revolution is too sacred, at least to us, to be so lightly used or misused. But if you say you are for the national revolution and the aims of your struggle is an Indian republic of the type of the United State of America, then I ask you to please let known on what forces you rely that will help you bring about that revolution. Whether national or the socialist, are the peasantry and the labour. Congress leaders do not dare to organize those forces. You have seen it in this movement. They know it better than anybody else that without these forces they are absolutely helpless. When they passed the resolution of complete independence – that really meant a revolution – they did not mean it. They had to do it under pressure of the younger element, and then they wanted to use it as a threat to achieve their hearts' desire – Dominion Status. You can easily judge it by studying the resolutions of the last three sessions of the Congress. I mean Madras, Calcutta and Lahore. At Calcutta, they passed a resolution asking for Dominion Status within twelve months, otherwise they would be forced to adopt complete independence as their object, and in all solemnity waited for some such gift till midnight after the 31st December, 1929. Then they found themselves "honour bound" to adopt the Independence resolution, otherwise they did not mean it. But even then Mahatmaji made no secret of the fact that the door (for compromise) was open. That was the real spirit. At the very outset they knew that their movement could not but end in some compromise. It is this half-heartedness that we hate, not the compromise at a particular stage in the struggle. Anyway, we were discussing the forces on which you can depend for a revolution. But if you say that you will approach the peasants and labourers to enlist their active support, let me tell you that they are not going to be fooled by any sentimental talk. They ask you quite candidly: what are they going to gain by your revolution for which you demand their sacrifices, what difference does it make to them whether Lord Reading is the head of the Indian government or

Sir Purshotamdas Thakordas? What difference for a peasant if Sir Tej Bahadur Sapru replaces Lord Irwin! It is useless to appeal to his national sentiment. You can't "use" him for your purpose; you shall have to mean seriously and to make him understand that the revolution is going to be his and for his good. The revolution of the proletariat and for the proletariat.

When you have formulated this clear-cut idea about your goals you can proceed in right earnest to organize your forces for such an action. Now there are two different phases through which you shall have to pass. First, the preparation; second, the action.

After the present movement ends, you will find disgust and some disappointment amongst the sincere revolutionary workers. But you need not worry. Leave sentimentalism aside. Be prepared to face the facts. Revolution is a very difficult task. It is beyond the power of any man to make a revolution. Neither can it be brought about on any appointed date. It is brought can it be brought about on an appointed date. It is brought about by special environments, social and economic. The function of an organized party is to utilise an such opportunity offered by these circumstances. And to prepare the masses and organize the forces for the revolution is a very difficult task. And that required a very great sacrifice on the part of the revolutionary workers. Let me make it clear that if you are a businessman or an established worldly or family man, please don't play with fire. As a leader you are of no use to the party. We have already very many such leaders who spare some evening hours for delivering speeches. They are useless. We require – to use the term so dear to Lenin – the "professional revolutionaries". The whole-time workers who have no other ambitions or life-work except the revolution. The greater the number of such workers organized into a party, the great the chances of your success.

To proceed systematically, what you need the most is a party with workers of the type discussed above with clear-cut ideas and keen perception and ability of initiative and quick decisions. The party shall have iron discipline and it need not necessarily be an underground party, rather the contrary. Thought the policy of voluntarily going to jail should altogether be abandoned. That will create a number of workers who shall be forced to lead an underground life. They should carry on the work with the same zeal. And it is this group of workers that shall produce worthy leaders for the real opportunity.

The party requires workers which can be recruited only through the youth movement. Hence we find the youth movement as the starting point of our programme. The youth movement should organize study circles, class lectures and publication of leaflets, pamphlets, books and periodicals. This is the best recruiting and training ground for political workers.

Those young men who may have matured their ideas and may find themselves ready to devote their life to the cause, may be transferred to the party. The party workers shall always guide and control the work of the youth movement as well. The party should start with the work of mass propaganda. It is very essential. One of the fundamental causes of the failure of the efforts of the Ghadar Party (1914-15) was the ignorance, apathy and sometimes active opposition of the masses. And apart from that, it is essential for gaining the active sympathy of and of and organising the peasants and workers. The name of party or rather, a communist party. This party of political workers, bound by strict discipline, should handle all other movements. It shall have to organize the peasants' and workers' parties, labour unions, and kindred political bodes. And in order to create political consciousness, not only of national politics but class politics as well, the party should organize a big publishing campaign. Subjects on all proletens [Original transcription is unclear – MIA Transcriber] enlightening the masses of the socialist theory shall be wit in easy reach and distributed widely. The writings should be simple and clear.

There are certain people in the labour movement who enlist some absurd ideas about the economic liberty of the peasants and workers without political freedom. They are demagogues or muddle-headed people. Such ideas are unimaginable and preposterous. We mean the economic liberty of the masses, and for that very purpose we are striving to win the political power. No doubt in the beginning, we shall have to fight for little economic demands and privileges of these classes. But these struggles are the best means for educating them for a final struggles are the best means for educating them for a final struggle to conquer political power.

Apart from these, there shall necessarily be organized a military department. This is very important. At times its need is felt very badly. But at that time you cannot start and formulate such a group with substantial means to act effectively. Perhaps this is the topic that needs a careful explanation. There is very great probability of my being misunderstood on this subject. Apparently I have acted like a terrorist. But I am not a terrorist. I am a revolutionary who has got such definite ideas of a lengthy programme as is being discussed here. My "comrades in arms" might accuse me, like Ram Prasad Bismil, for having been subjected to certain sort of reaction in the condemned cell, which is not true. I have got the same ideas, same convictions, same convictions, same zeal and same spirit as I used to have outside, perhaps – nay, decidedly – better. Hence I warn my readers to be careful while reading my words. They should not try to read anything between the lines. Let me announced with all the strength at my command, that I am not a terrorist and I never was, expected perhaps in the beginning of my revolutionary career. And I am convinced that we cannot gain anything through those methods. One can easily judge it from the history of the Hindustan Socialist Republican Association. All our activities were directed towards an aim, i.e., identifying ourselves with the great movement as its military wing. If anybody has misunderstood me, let him amend his ideas. I do not mean that bombs and pistols are useless, rather the contrary. But I mean to say that mere bomb-throwing is not only useless but sometimes harmful. The military department of the party should always keep ready all the war-material it can command for any emergency. It should back the political work of the party. It cannot and should not work independently.

On these lines indicated above, the party should proceed with its work. Through periodical meetings and conferences they should go on educating and enlightening their workers on all topics. If you start the work on these lines, you shall have to be very sober. The programme requires at least twenty years for its fulfillment. Cast aside the youthful dreams of a revolution within ten years of Gandhi's utopian promises of Swaraj in One Year. It requires neither the emotion nor the death, but the life of constant struggle, suffering and sacrifice. Crush your individuality first. Shake off the dreams of personal comfort. Then start to work. Inch by inch you shall have to proceed. It needs courage, perseverance and very strong determination. No difficulties and no hardships shall discourage you. No failure and betrayals shall dishearten you. No travails (!) imposed upon you shall snuff out the revolutionary will in you. Through the ordeal of sufferings and sacrifice you shall come out victorious. And these individual victories shall be the valuable assets of the revolution.

LONG LIVE REVOLUTION

2nd February, 1931

Regarding Line of Defence in Hari Kishan's Case

June, 1931

[On December 23, 1930, when the Government of Punjab was coming out of the University Hall, Lahore, after delivering his convocation address, Hari Kishan fired at him. One man died and the Governor was slightly injured. During the trial Hari Kishan's defence counsel took the line that Hari Kishan had no intention to kill the Governor and that he only wanted to give a warning.

Bhagat Singh was opposed to this line of defence. He wrote to one of his friends outside about how revolutionary cases should be conducted. This letter was published in the people in June 1931.]

I AM VERY SORRY TO NOTE THAT MY LAST LETTER in this connection did not reach its destination at the proper time and therefore could be of no use, or failed to serve the purpose or which it was written. Hence, I write this letter to let you know my views on the question of defence in the political cases in general and the revolutionary cases in particular. Apart from certain points already discussed in that letter, it shall serve another purpose too, i.e. it shall be a documentary proof that I am not becoming wise after the event.

Anyhow, I wrote in that letter that the plea that the lawyer was suggestion to offer defence, should not be adopted. But it has been done in spite of your, and mine, opposition. Nevertheless, we can now discuss the matter in a better light and can formulate definite Ideas about the future policy regarding defence.

You know that I have never been in favour of defending all the political accused. But this does not imply that the beauty of the real struggle should be altogether spoiled. (Please note that the term beauty is not used in the abstract sense but it means the motive that actuated a particular action). When I say that all the politicals should always defend themselves, I say it with certain reservations. It can be cleared by just one explanation. A man does an act with a certain end in view. After his arrest the political significance of the action should not be diminished. The perpetrator should not become more important than the action itself. Let us further elucidate it with the help of the illustration. Mr. Hari Kishan came to shoot the Governor. I don't want only to discuss the ethical side of the action. I want only to discuss the political side of the case. The man was arrested. Unfortunately, some police official had died in the action. Now comes the question of the defence; well, when fortunately the Governor had escaped there could be a very beautiful statement in his case, i.e., the statement of actual facts as was made in the lower court. And it would have served the legal purpose too. The wisdom and ability of the lawyer depended on his interpretation of the cause of the Sub-Inspector's death. What did he gain by saying that he did not intend to kill the Governor and only wanted to warn him, and all that sort of thing? Can any sensible man imagine even for a moment the possibility of such a design? Had it any legal value? Absolutely none. Then, what was the use of spoiling the beauty of not only the particular action but also the general movement? Warning and futile protests cannot go on forever. The warning has once been given long ago. The revolutionary struggle had begun in right earnest so far as the strength of the revolutionary party allowed. Viceroy's train action was neither a test nor a warning. Similarly, Mr. Hari Kishan's action was part of the struggle itself, not a warning. After the failure of the action, the accused can take it in purely sportman-like spirit. The purpose having been served he ought to have rejoiced in the lucky escape of the Governor. There is no use of killing any one individual. These actions have their political significance in as much as they serve to create a mentality and an atmosphere which shall be very necessary to the final struggle. That is all. Individual actions are to win the moral support of the people. We sometimes designate them as the 'propaganda through deed'.

Now, the people should be defended but subject to the above consideration. This is after all a common principle that all the contending parties always try to gain more and to lose less. No general can ever adopt a policy in which he may have to make a greater sacrifice than the gain expected. Nobody would be more anxious to save the precious life of Mr. Hari Kishan than myself. But I want to let you know that the thing which makes his life precious should by no means be ignored. To save the lives at any cost, is not our policy. It may be the policy of the easy-chair politicians, but it is not ours.

Much of the defence policy depends upon the mentality of the accused himself. But if the accused himself is not only afraid of shrinking but is as enthusiastic as ever, than his work for which he risked his life should be considered first, his personal question afterwards. Again, there may be some sort of confusion. There may be cases where the action is of no general importance in spite of its tremendous local value. There the accused should not be sentimental as to admit the responsibility. The famous trial of Nirmal Kant Rai would be the best illustration.

But in cases like the where it is of such political importance, the personal aspect should not be attached greater value than the political one. If you want to know my frank opinion about his case, let me tell you frankly that it is nothing short of the political murder of an incident of historic importance at the altar o professional (legal) vanity.

Here I may point out one thing more, that the people responsible for this strangulation of the case, having realized their blunder and having become wise after the event in not daring to shoulder their responsibility, are trying to belittle the beauty of the marvelous character of our young comrade. I have heard them saying that Mr. Hari Kishan shirked to face it boldly.

This is a most shame-faced lie. He is the most courageous led I have ever come across. People should have mercy upon us. Better ignored than demoralized and degraded but well looked after.

Lawyers should not be so unscrupulous as to exploit the lives and even deaths of young people who come to sacrifice themselves for so noble a cause as the emancipation of the suffering humanity. I am really...[8], Otherwise, why should a lawyer demand such an incredible fee as has been paid in the above case?

In the sedition cases, I may tell you the limit to which we can allow the defence. Last year when one comrade was prosecuted for having delivered a socialistic speech and when he pleaded not guilty to that charge, we were simply astounded. In such cases we should demand the right of free speech. But where such things are attributed to one a he has not said and are contrary to the interests of the movement, deny. Thought in the present movement

8. Here some words are evidently missing.

the Congress has suffered for having allowed its members to go to jail without defending themselves, in my opinion that was a mistake.

Anyhow, I think if you read this letter along with my previous one, you will come to know very clearly my ideas about the defence in political cases. In Mr. Hari Kishan's case, in my opinion, his appeal should be filed in the High Court without fail and every effort should be made to save him.

I hope both these letters indicate everything I want to say on this subject.

Bhagat Singh's Last Petition

1930

To,
The Punjab Governor

Sir,

With due respect we beg to bring to your kind notice the following:

That we were sentenced to death on 7th October 1930 by a British Court, L.C.C Tribunal, constituted under the Sp. Lahore Conspiracy Case Ordinance, promulgated by the H.E. The Viceroy, the Head of the British Government of India, and that the main charge against us was that of having waged war against H.M. King George, the King of England.

The above-mentioned finding of the Court pre-supposed two things:

Firstly, that there exists a state of war between the British Nation and the Indian Nation and, secondly, that we had actually participated in that war and were therefore war prisoners.

The second pre-supposition seems to be a little bit flattering, but nevertheless it is too tempting to resist the desire of acquiescing in it.

As regards the first, we are constrained to go into some detail. Apparently there seems to be no such war as the phrase indicates. Nevertheless, please allow us to accept the validity of the pre-supposition taking it at its face value. But in order to be correctly understood we must explain it further. Let us declare that the state of war does exist and shall exist so long as the Indian toiling masses and the natural resources are being exploited by a handful of parasites. They may be purely British Capitalist or mixed British and Indian or even purely Indian. They may be carrying on their insidious exploitation through mixed or even on purely Indian bureaucratic apparatus. All these things make no difference. No matter, if your Government tries and succeeds in winning over the leaders of the upper strata of the Indian Society through petty concessions and compromises and thereby cause a temporary demoralization in the main body of the forces. No matter, if once again the vanguard of the Indian movement, the Revolutionary Party, finds itself deserted in the thick of the war. No matter if the leaders to whom personally we are much indebted for the sympathy and feelings they expressed for us, but nevertheless we cannot overlook the fact that they did become so callous as to ignore and not to make a mention in the peace negotiation of even the homeless, friendless and penniless of female workers who are alleged to be belonging to the vanguard and whom the leaders consider to be enemies of their utopian non-violent cult which has already become a thing of the past; the heroines who had ungrudgingly sacrificed or offered for sacrifice their husbands, brothers, and all that were nearest and dearest to them, including themselves, whom your government has declared to be outlaws. No matter, it your agents stoop so low as to fabricate baseless calumnies against their spotless characters to damage their and their party's reputation. The war shall continue.

It may assume different shapes at different times. It may become now open, now hidden, now purely agitational, now fierce life and death struggle. The choice of the course, whether bloody or comparatively peaceful, which it should adopt rests with you. Choose whichever you like. But that war shall be incessantly waged without taking into consideration the petty (illegible) and the meaningless ethical ideologies. It shall be waged ever with new vigour, greater audacity and unflinching determination till the Socialist Republic is established and the present social order is completely replaced by a new social order, based on social prosperity and thus every sort of exploitation is put an end to and the humanity is ushered into the era of genuine and permanent peace. In the very near future the final battle shall be fought and final settlement arrived at.

The days of capitalist and imperialist exploitation are numbered. The war neither began with us nor is it going to end with our lives. It is the inevitable consequence of the historic events and the existing environments. Our humble sacrifices shall be only a link in the chain that has very accurately been beautified by the unparalleled sacrifice of Mr. Das and most tragic but noblest sacrifice of Comrade Bhagawati Charan and the glorious death of our dear warrior Azad.

As to the question of our fates, please allow us to say that when you have decided to put us to death, you will certainly do it. You have got the power in your hands and the power is the greatest justification in this world. We know that the maxim "Might is right" serves as your guiding motto. The whole of our trial was just a proof of that. We wanted to point out that according to the verdict of your court we had waged war and were therefore war prisoners. And we claim to be treated as such, i.e., we claim to be shot dead instead of to be hanged. It rests with you to prove that you really meant what your court has said.

We request and hope that you will very kindly order the military department to send its detachment to perform our execution.

Yours,

Bhagat Singh

OTHER HARDBACK BOOKS

- 1984 by George Orwell
  Fiction/Classics, ISBN: 9788193545836
- Abraham Lincoln by Lord Charnwood
  Biographies/Leaders, ISBN: 9789387669147
- Alice's Adventures in Wonderland by Lewis Carroll
  Children's/Classics, ISBN: 9789387669055
- Animal Farm by George Orwell
  Fiction/Classics, ISBN: 9789387669062
- Anthem by Ayn Rand
  Fiction/Classics, ISBN: 9789389157178
- As a Man Thinketh by James Allen
  Fiction/Classics, ISBN: 9789388118422
- Awakened Imagination by Neville Goddard
  Religion & Spirituality, ISBN: 9789389157185
- Be What You Wish by Neville Goddard
  Mind, Body & Spirit, ISBN: 9789388118163
- Becoming a Writer by Dorothea Brande
  Self Help/General, ISBN: 9789389157192
- Believe in Yourself by Joseph Murphy
  Mind, Body & Spirit, ISBN: 9789388118439
- Black Beauty by Anna Sewell
  Children's/Classics, ISBN: 9789388118262
- Civilization and Its Discontents by Sigmund Freud
  Social Sciences/General, ISBN: 9789388118279
- Demian by Hermann Hesse
  Fiction/Classics, ISBN: 9789388118170
- Feeling is the Secret by Neville Goddard
  Religion & Spirituality, ISBN: 9789389157208

Search the book by its ISBN

OTHER HARDBACK BOOKS

- Gitanjali by Rabindranath Tagore
  Fiction/Poems, ISBN: 9789387669079
- Great Speeches of Abraham Lincoln by Abraham Lincoln
  History/United States, ISBN: 9789387669154
- How to Attract Money by Joseph Murphy
  Self Help/Success, ISBN: 9789388118446
- How to be Filled with the Holy Spirit by A.W. Tozer
  Religion/Christianity, ISBN: 9789389157215
- How to Enjoy Your Life and Your Job by Dale Carnegie
  Self Help/General, ISBN: 9789388118293
- Illust. Biography of William Shakespeare by Manju Gupta
  Biographies/Authors, ISBN: 9789387669246
- Madhubala by Manju Gupta
  Biographies/Cinems, ISBN: 9789387669253
- Mansarover 1 (Hindi) by Premchand
  Fiction/Short Stories, ISBN: 9789387669086
- Meditations by Marcus Aurelius
  Non Fiction/Philosopy, ISBN: 9789388118781
- My Inventions: The Autobio. of Nikola Tesla by Nikola Tesla
  Autobiographies/Scientists, ISBN: 9789388118187
- Selected Stories of Rabindranath Tagore by Rabindranath Tagore
  Fiction/Short Stories, ISBN: 9789387669307
- Sense and Sensibility by Jane Austen
  Fiction/Classics, ISBN: 9789387669109
- Siddhartha by Hermann Hesse
  Fiction/Classics, ISBN: 9789387669116
- Tales from India by Rudyard Kipling
  Fiction/Short Stories, ISBN: 9789387669123

Search the book by its ISBN

OTHER HARDBACK BOOKS

- Tales from Shakespeare by Charles Lamb, Mary Lamb
  Fiction/Short Stories, ISBN: 9789387669314
- The Alchemy of Happiness by Al-Ghazzali
  Religion & Spirituality, ISBN: 9789388118309
- The Art of Public Speaking by Dale Carnegie
  Self Help/General, ISBN: 9789388118477
- The Autobiography of a Yogi by Paramahansa Yogananda
  Autobiographies/General, ISBN: 9789387669192
- The Dynamic Laws of Prosperity by Catherine Ponder
  Mind, Body & Spirit, ISBN: 9789388118194
- The Elements of Style by William Strunk
  Non Fiction/Skill, ISBN: 9789389157222
- The Game of Life and How to Play It by Florence Scovel Shinn
  Mind, Body & Spirit, ISBN: 9789388118316
- The Imitation of Christ by Thomas À Kempis
  Religion/Christianity, ISBN: 9789388118200
- The Jungle Book by Rudyard Kipling
  Children's/Classics, ISBN: 9789387669338
- The Knowledge of the Holy by A.W. Tozer
  Religion/Christianity, ISBN: 9789389157239
- The Light of Asia by Sir Edwin Arnold
  Fiction/Poetry, ISBN: 9789387669130
- The Magic of Faith by Joseph Murphy
  Mind, Body & Spirit, ISBN: 9789388118712
- The Origin of Species by Charles Darwin
  Sciences/Life Sciences, ISBN: 9789387669345
- The Path of Prosperity by James Allen
  Mind, Body & Spirit, ISBN: 9789388118323

Search the book by its ISBN

OTHER HARDBACK BOOKS

- The Power of Awareness by Neville Goddard
  Mind, Body & Spirit, ISBN: 9789388118330
- The Power of Concentration by Theron Q. Dumont
  Self Help/General, ISBN: 9789388118224
- The Power of Positive Thinking by Norman Vincent Peale
  Mind, Body & Spirit, ISBN: 9789388118729
- The Prophet by Kahlil Gibran
  Fiction/Classics, ISBN: 9789388118453
- The Psychopathology of Everyday Life by Sigmund Freud
  Non Fiction/Psychology, ISBN: 9789388118231
- The Pursuit of God by A.W. Tozer
  Religion/Christianity, ISBN: 9789389157246
- The Quick and Easy Way to Effec. Speaking by Dale Carnegie
  Self Help/General, ISBN: 9789388118347
- The Science of Getting Rich by Wallace D. Wattles
  Self Help/Success, ISBN: 9789387669239
- The Seven Laws of Teaching by John Milton Gregory
  Self Help/General, ISBN: 9789388118460
- The Upanishads by Swami Paramananda
  Religion/Hinduism, ISBN: 9789388118774
- The World as I See It by Albert Einstein
  Non Fiction/Philosopy, ISBN: 9789388118248
- Thought Vibration by William Walker Atkinson
  Non Fiction/Philosopy, ISBN: 9789389157253
- Wake Up and Live! by Dorothea Brande
  Mind, Body & Spirit, ISBN: 9789388118255
- Your Faith is Your Fortune by Neville Goddard
  Religion & Spirituality, ISBN: 9789389157260

Search the book by its ISBN